Teaching of Social Studies

Published by
Lotus Press Publishers & Distributors

Teaching of Social Studies

R.K. Sharma

LOTUS PRESS
4735/22, Prakash Deep Building,
Ansari Road, Daryaganj,
New Delhi - 110002

Lotus Press Publishers & Distributors
Unit No.220, 2nd Floor, 4735/22, Prakash Deep Building,
Ansari Road, Daryaganj, New Delhi - 110002
Ph.: 32903912, 23280047, 09811838000
E-mail : lotus_press@sify.com
Visit us : www.lotuspress.co.in

Teaching of Social Studies

ISBN: 81-8382-113-8

Published by : **Lotus Press Publishers & Distributors**, New Delhi-110002
Printed at : **A.J. Book Binding House**, Delhi

PREFACE

Teaching of Social Studies is a complete text-cum-reference book for teachers, teacher-trainers, and teacher-trainees of all pedagogical institutes and departments of Education of different universities.

The present book is designed to highlight the important aspects of nature, scope, features, functions and aims of teaching about the said subject. In the chapters of this book guidance regarding curriculum, audio-visual aids, laboratory and text books, teaching planning has been given in a very impressive manner. This book can prove an effective guide to teachers and teacher-trainees for understanding the psychology of students and their problems and show the right path in the field of teaching.

This book deals with the topics of Social Studies—Nature, Scope, Features and Functions; Aims and Methods, of Social Studies; Curriculum and Contents; Audio-Visual Aids in Teaching; Community Resources, Laboratory and Text Books; Teacher and Lesson Planning; Evaluation in Social Studies etc.

All the fundamentals of Teaching of Social Studies has been given in this book which have been drawn from authoritative sources. Yet the simple interpretation makes it an ideal text-cum-reference book.

I am thankful to various authors and educational researchers whose works are consulted, cited or reproduced here. Last but not the least, I owe a deep sense of gratitude to my publisher for materialising my present endeavour.

EDITOR

Contents

1

Social Studies—Nature, Scope, Features and Functions

According to J.F. Forrester, "Social Studies studies the society." In this way, social studies mean to study the society in terms of its various activities. It is a study of the relationship between man and society. Generally speaking this subject includes material of all social sciences which help in, development of social sciences and for social efficiency. So, in Social Studies, subject matter relating to History, Political Science, Geography, Economics and Sociology is included. From these subjects only that material is taken up which is beneficial for the social development of the child. Different subjects are integrated in such a way that Social Studies becomes entirely a new subject. Different scholars have defined it as under.

According to M. Forrester, "Social Studies, as the very name suggests is the study of society and its chief aim is to help pupils to understand the world in which they live and how it came to be, so that they may become responsible citizens."

According to Jarolemek, "Social Studies deal with the study of man and his relationships with other man and with his environment."

According to Bining and Bining, "Those (Studies) whose subject matter relates directly to the organisation and development of human society and, to man as a member of social group."

According to John U. Micheals, "The Social Studies programme is the study of man and his interaction with the social and physical environment in the past, present and emerging future."

Above definitions clearly point out that 'man' is the central point in Social Studies. It studies man's struggle against the environment for the existence of mankind. The following characteristics become apparent on the basis of these definitions.

1. It studies man and the associations which help in developing responsible citizens.
2. The study of this subject conforms that men in the entire world are mutually dependent, in economic and political terms and they spend life together at local, national and international levels.
3. It is the study of social institutions with regard to their origin and development.
4. It is a study which helps to explain and interpret to the pupils that environment in which they are born and have developed.
5. It studies interaction between man and his environment. At the same time it studies the social and other kinds of environment.
6. It explains the impact of world events on our day to day life.
7. It studies facts, problems and patterns which affected humanity in past and in present.
8. It helps in explaining the present world civilisation and in understanding contemporary problems.
9. In social studies it is not only coordinated treatment, but also an integrated approach.

Nature and Scope of Social Studies. Social Studies draws its material from the various social sciences such as History, Geography, Economics, Civics, Political Science, Philosophy, Sociology, Public Administration, etc. But it is not history plus geography plus economics, etc.—a chunk from here and a chunk from there. It integrates the material of all these sciences in one conglomeration. That is why, it is called, 'coordinated and coordinating by nature'. Social Studies consists of a fresh arrangement and different treatment for the purpose of achieving certain ends, described as social ends. We have all along been teaching history, geography, civics, economics as separate subjects. Now this practice seems to be unsound and incomplete. Certain topics, not forming a part of the traditional curricula of history, geography, civics and economics, will not be found in the new curriculum of Social Studies. It is not much the difference of contents but it is the different approach and aims that is meant to be achieved. Social Studies are part of the modern approach to education which aims at forming standards, attitudes, ideals and interests rather than the accumulation of factual information.

Wide Scope. Social Studies provides a wide range of materials. It involves numerous skills and leads to generalisations, which will naturally challenge the varied capacities of our students. Its scope is really very wide and its theme is the present social life of may the world over.

Course is not Limitless. But it does not mean that Social Studies course is a limitless and fathomless ocean. Its frontiers have to be demarcated so as to provide an over-all integrated outline of essential common knowledge only. It draws the functional knowledge from various subjects and avoids the material which has no bearing on social context., Thus, the subject matter of Social Studies will consist of only reorganised, simplified and purposely selected items of information and experience from various fields which have a practical bearing on daily lives of children. The principle of 'minimum essentials' is followed throughout.

Social Studies, as we find it, is formed mainly of three subjects Geography, History, and Civics. It also includes the elements of Economics, Sociology, Ethics, Anthropology, etc.

Geography. Geography literally means description of the earth. But there are a number of things on this earth and it is not possible to describe all these phenomena taking place on the surface of this earth. The problem arises as to what to describe and what to omits? Man concerned with earth, as earth is the home of man. Geography studies the home of man or the study of physical environment of man, particularly in its relation to human activities. The factors in physical environment which have a definite influence on human life are more important in geography than those which have little or no influence. It studies adjustment of human group to their physical environment. Geography studies the interaction of man with his environments. Geography aims at training future young citizens to imagine accurately the conditions of the great world and to help them to think clearly about economic and social problems of the world around.

History. History is the first and foremost branch of Social Studies. It is as old as the human race itself. History dealt with political and military affairs, stressing wars especially. Not much mention was made of the social, political or moral state and conditions of the society. History was neither of the country nor of the people but it was of the kings, queens and warriors. The changes in social outlook and political life, introduction of democratic ideals and institutions all led to the extension of the boundaries of history taught in the schools. After that it was made to include social, economic, industrial, scientific and cultural aspects in addition to the political phases and it has been made interpretative rather than merely descriptive. Because of this, it has occupied pivotal place in Social Studies programme in our schools. The aim is not to train memory faculty of the child but to impart him civic and social training. It showed aim at teaching the child the history of his own land and people, the life in the past and trends of progress of our present society.

Civics. The importance of its inclusion in Social Studies has been recently realised with the rise of political awakening and the dawn of freedom. Its knowledge helps to understand present day society its very complex institutions and efforts to better the society. This subject aims to give an idea of the organisation, structure and function of the political and civic institutions. Thus, each social science describes and explains some aspects of human relationship. For example history, part of Social Studies, explains the record of man's successes and failures in course of march of civilization. Geography on the other hand, describes man's relationships to his physical environment. Civics describes the forms and types of governments and their functions. Thus, various social sciences are closely related around human relationship. It is, therefore, natural for them to find a common designation for subjects with common elements. Thus, the term Social Studies became the collective name for the instructional materials drawn from these and concerned with human relationships, just as the social sciences became a collective term.

"The purpose of Social Studies in schools is social initiation or the development of social character by drawing the individual into the community and making him aware of its collective life and collective ideals." Social awareness is very essential to avoid anti-social influences like greed, selfishness, intolerance, etc. Subjects like History, Geography, Civics and Economics, etc. also develop social awareness but their effect is only one-sided as against through an integrated course of Social Studies.

It may be concluded from the scope, as explained above, that Social Studies provides a wide range of materials. It involves numerous skills and leads to generalisations, which will naturally challenge the various capacities of our children. Its scope is really very wide and its theme is the present social life of man the world over. But it does not mean that Social Studies course is a limitless and fathomless ocean. Its frontiers have to be compressed so as to provide an over-all integrated outline of essential common knowledge only. It draws only the functional knowledge from various social sciences and avoids and ignores the contents which have got no social bearing. Thus, the subject-matter of Social Studies consists of only reorganised, simplified and purposely selected items of information and experience from various fields which have a practical bearing on the daily lives of our children. The principle of minimum essential is followed throughout.

The following questions may confront every teacher of Social Studies. What is Social Studies and why should we teach this subject in place of History, Geography, Economics, Civics, etc.. The term 'Social Sciences' and 'Social Studies' are used is interchangeably in regard to social subjects taught in the secondary schools. The commission of the American Historical Association on Social Studies thus stated.

"The Social Sciences, more than any other discipline of the school curriculum, are concerned immediately with the life, the institution, the thought, the aspirations and the far reaching policies of the nation in the world setting. The Social Sciences take as their providence, the entire range of human history from the earliest time down to the latest moment and the widest reaches of contemporary society from the life and customs of the most remote people to the Social parties and cultural possessions of the immediate neighbourhood. The Social Sciences, thus, embrace the traditional disciplines which are concerned directly with man and society."

The life and activities of the people provide the subject-matter for the various social sciences which have been organised into such subjects as History, Civics, Economics, Geography, Sociology, Anthropology, etc.

The subject-matter of Social sciences taught in the school known as 'Social Studies' draws its material from History, Geography, Civics, Economics, etc. They consist of a fresh arrangement and different treatment for the purpose of achieving certain ends, earlier described as social ends. We have all along been teaching History, Geography, Civics and Economics as separate subjects. Now this practice seems to be unsound and incomplete Certain topics, not forming a part of the traditional curricula of History, Geography, Economics and Civics and certain topic of the old will not be found in the new curriculum of Social Studies. It is not much the difference of contents but it is the different approach and aims that is aimed to be achieved. Social Studies are part of the modern approach to education which aim at forming standards, attitudes, ideals and interest rather than accumulation of factual information. Today no one will dispute that an education which gives information as to right action but fails to inspire the students with a desire to do it is failing in its objective, Education is to teach people to do and enjoy right things. It is a subject which helps to lead a better life in a society and also helps in developing a balanced personality of the child. It aims at making every child a worthy citizen. It also helps the students to develop the ability to use knowledge of facts, principles of Social Studies in specific life situations.

Hereunder are given some justification for the teaching of Social Studies in our schools.

1. Education wants to prepare a child for successful and effective living. It deals exclusively with man's problems. It is the only discipline which provide experiences and interprets life, particularly social life.
2. Social Studies is more concerned with life situation than with formal studies and it widens the outlook of the students.
3. History, Geography, Economics and Civics were providing formal type of education. The Result was the failure in explaining the social environment to the school children in a comprehensive manner.
4. It emphasizes the development of the whole personality of the student. It helps to develop correct and right attitudes, interests, independent thinking and acquisition of social information.
5. It develops a spirit of tolerance, sympathy and love for one's country by removing the prejudices.
6. It awakens social consciousness and promotes national integration and international understanding among the students.
7. It helps the students to develop healthy outlook, cooperative spirit, love for own and other cultures and heritage of mankind.

Thus, we can say that Social Studies should have a prominent place in the present educational set up instead of teaching social sciences as separate subjects.

MAIN FEATURES OF SOCIAL STUDIES

1. Compound Rather than Mixture. Social Studies is a compound rather than a mixture in which the ingredients lose their identity and something new emerges out of the combination. Social studies differs from teaching of History, Geography, Economics, Civics, etc. The subject areas which constitute it, acquire a new meaning and assume a new dimension.

2. Study of the Web of Social Relationships. It is the study of the web of relationships that develop between and among people and between people and their environment. It deals with individuals only for the purpose of securing additional light on the larger social realities, classes, groups, institutions, traditions and organisations. Intellectual and social skills and attitudes relevant to the understanding of some aspects of social living are developed. Social Studies seeks to describe and analyse the effects of Work in mines, in factories, on farms and on people living on a mountain, a sea and a desert.

3. Socio-Economic Central Theme. The central theme of Social Studies is socio-economic and occupational usefulness. Its main object is to prepare the child for wholesome social living. The child begins to appreciate the geographical elements of his environment and to understand how the gifts of nature are processed to produce goods for serving the various needs of man. He gets an idea of the social and cultural life in different parts of the country and the world. He gets opportunities to develop socially desirable habits, attitudes and values and becomes broadly acquainted with the functioning of political and social institutions.

4. Realistic Course. Real life situations are the laboratories of such social studies concepts as interaction, cooperation and interdependence. It studies the problems and processes man faces, as he carries on his basic activities.

5. Inter-disciplinary Social Science. Social Studies is a broad and composite inter-disciplinary social science which draws its information from different social sciences to unfold the total environment of the child with special reference to the physical, social and cultural elements. It helps in the study of historical, geographical and local relations and inter-relations.

6. Commitment to Action. Through their content and teaching methods Social Studies help the student to learn the processes of individual and group action of citizens in a democracy. Through participation in class, school and community activities, students learn how a democratic society functions. Learning the skills and behaviour patterns required in a democratic situation, they develop a commitment to democratic means for solving problems.

7. Human Study. Social studies focus on folks, not on the technical processes or the machines. For example, in order to study Man's increasing control on power resources takes his class to visit a Power Project. Here, he will explain the likely effects of bringing electricity to the village on the lives of his pupils and their parents. This is because social studies deal not with machines or technical processes but with people, men and women, boys and girls and their inter-relationships.

SOCIAL SCIENCES

According io Charles Beard Social sciences are a body of knowledge and thought pertaining to human affairs as distinguished from sticks, stones, stars and physical objects. James High defines the Social Sciences as those bodies of learning and study which recognise the simultaneous and mutual action of physical and non-physical stimuli which produce social reaction.

Social sciences include history, geography, political science, economics, anthropology and sociology which represent man's fundamental needs: the human record, habitat, political structure, subsistence, human derivation and social organisation. Human or cultural geography and psychology account for human needs of acceptance and personal adjustment. Social Sciences may also include social biology, ethics, philosophy, jurisprudence, statistics, linguistics and education, and even rhetoric, logic and grammar.

Classification. According to James High the most easily classifiable Social Sciences are: Psychology (man's mind), Anthropology (man's ethos), Geography (man's abode), Economics (man's subsistence), Political Science (man's order), Sociology (man's associations) and History (man's story). All these are individual disciplines of investigation having sufficient independent bodies of subject-matter.

Characteristics

1. Direct Bearing on Man's Activities—Social Sciences are those parts of cultural knowledge, which have direct bearing on man's activities in specific field.
2. Advanced Studies of human society—Social Sciences are the advanced studies of human society taught to maturer students.
3. Truth providing objective—Social Sciences seek to find out new truths about human relationships to contribute to social utility and advancement of knowledge.

Social Sciences and Social Studies. Both focus on man's relationship, both these have a common way of content to man and to his environment. But while social sciences represent an adult approach, social studies is child-centred.

Social Studies is a Subject that Deals with Human Relationships

It is an all-embracing subject which touches all aspects of human life. It embraces material related to human relationships drawn from History, Geography, Political Science, Economics, Civics, Sociology, Social Psychology, Philosophy, etc. Its functional material is sifted from all these and is fused and unified into one field called Social Studies.

Social Studies not a Combination of Social Sciences

Social Studies is not a combination of Social Sciences like History, Geography, Civics, Economics, etc. Though Social Studies draws its material from History, Geography, Civics, Economics etc, but it is not a part of History, Geography, Civics and Economics, put together unrelatedly.

It is not a combination of many subjects. It is one independent field of study which provides a core of knowledge, experience and insight around which other subjects, may be built up in a coordinated way. It draws functional and practical knowledge from various social sciences.

DISTINCTION OF SOCIAL STUDIES AND SOCIAL SCIENCES

1. Distinction in Nature. Social sciences provide detailed knowledge about their respective fields, written for adults while Social Studies is primarily designed for instructional purposes in schools. Social Sciences maintain a certain standard of scholarship not easily understood by school children. Social Studies is the simplified and reorganised form of social sciences. It is simple, easy, appealing, interesting and learnable.

2. Distinction in Viewpoint. Social sciences deal with theoretical aspect of human affairs, while Social Studies deals with the practical aspect. While Social sciences provide the theory in the respective fields; Social Studies is an integrated course made after sifting out the functional and practical material out of these.

3. Distinction in Aim. The aim of social sciences is theoretical study while that of Social Studies practically utility. The aim of social sciences is to provide knowledge whereas that of Social Studies is to develop individuals into good citizens.

4. Distinction in Readers. Social sciences may be studied by a chosen few while Social Studies is a must for everybody: While Social sciences deal with advanced knowledge, required for those only who pursue university education, Social Studies enables the people to become good citizens.

5. Distinction in Integration. Social sciences provide knowledge in isolated form whereas Social Studies provides integrated knowledge. Social sciences study society after analysing it into various aspects: giving knowledge in an isolated form. As the study of society as a unity, Social Studies provides an integrated of knowledge of society by drawing practical and functional knowledge out of social sciences and unifying it into one subject.

6. Distinction in Complexity. Social sciences are a complex study; whereas Social Studies is comparatively simple and easy. As advanced and detailed studies Social sciences are complex and difficult: Meant to be studied upto the higher secondary classes, Social Studies is practical and useful for everybody. It is simple and easy.

7. Distinction in Utility. Social sciences seek social utility Social Studies seeks instructional utility. In the words of Martorella, "It is more accurate to think of social studies as an applied field which attempts to fuse scientific knowledge with ethical, philosophical, religious and social considerations which arise in the process of decision-making as practised by the citizen."

8. Distinction in Scope. The scope of Social sciences is limited to their own field; whereas the scope of Social Studies is almost unlimited. As each social science studies its own field, its scope is limited. On the other hand, as the subject of Social Studies is all embracing in the sense that it concerns and touches all aspects of human life; its scope is almost unlimited.

To conclude, there is no hard and fast line separating social sciences and social studies. Social studies is to be taught at the primary classes, where gradual unfoldment of the total environment—physical, social, and cultural is needed. After the student becomes a competent investigator and interpreter of raw data in the Middle and Secondary stages he may now rise from the social studies to the study of social sciences.

Status of Social Studies

An important part of the core curriculum, Social Studies is taught as a part of the study of the environment in classes I and II and as the independent subject of social studies in subsequent classes.

Environmental studies include both natural and social environment in classes I and II. The term social studies rather than the social sciences will be used at the primary stage. To be taught upto primary classes Social studies represents a broad and composite instructional area drawing the information from different social sciences as History, Geography, Civics etc. to unfold the total environment of the child gradually with reference to the physical, social and cultural elements. It uses an integrated approach. It builds on the experiences of the child before he comes to school Social studies branches out to ever expanding horizons to include the world. For classes VI to VIII, Social studies programme is composed of separate courses in Indian History, the Geography of India, and the world, and Elementary Civics. In classes IX and X various subjects will be taught as independent disciplines, followed by the integrated approach. A systematic learning of the middle stage will be made use of recognising the ability of the older children at this stage to relate ideas to meaningful concepts and then to make generalisations, to act "courageously and with integrity.... consistent with democratic ideals and processes."

Why not Separate Subjects at the Secondary School Stage?

For the past several years there has been a steady movement against the separate teaching of social subjects like history, geography, civics and economics etc. at the secondary school stage. Instead a unified course of social studies is recommended to be introduced through the fusion of elements from various Social sciences. Social Studies course is built around a series of broad topics intended to introduce the young child to his physical and social environment. Following are the reasons. Why should we not teach history, geography, civics and economic separately at the secondary stage:

1. Same Social Concepts and Skills. As these subjects have the same social concepts and skills any knowledge given to school children in isolation cannot be easily understood and grasped by them. As children are not interested in disconnected ideas, offered by a number of subjects, it is better to give only a few important ideas, with all possible combinations. This will not over-burden the child with so many subjects.

2. General or Liberal Education. Upto secondary school stage is to give only general or liberal education. As this is the final or conclusive stage of education for the majority of children therefore the teacher should widen their vision and outlook on life as a whole, so that they may play an effective part as democratic citizens. This is possible only through an integrated course of social studies which includes the knowledge of physical, cultural, economic, social and civic experiences of man as well the development of attitudes and skills.

3. Need of Changed Outlook. When taught in isolation separate social sciences like history, geography, civics, economics and sociology fail to give an integrated knowledge of the social problems of everyday life. The students are hard-pressed under the burden of so many subjects and books, without knowing their utility in their daily life. They cannot acquaint themselves with the immediate problems of nation, society or the world which influence their daily life in one way or the other. Social sciences when taught separately, provide only partial and limited knowledge. History emphasises only the performances of certain individuals in different periods. Geography, when taught in isolation, describes only boundaries, locations and names of important cities, mountains, oceans and rivers without explaining their effect upon human life. Civics deals only with the structure and functions of government and not the activities and functions of various social groups like the school, the family, the local community, the village community and the nation. Economics emphasises only abstract theories and definitions and the ethics of earning and using wealth, not the social nature of economic activity.

4. Need of Total Education. In former times the small communities provided the child with rich activities enabling him to learn inter-personal relationship of the group. Through the daily experiences of his life he became fully aware of the relationship that existed between himself and his environment. His family and his community gave him all the social education that he required. Today, our community has become larger and more complex due to various scientific inventions, developed means of communication and transport and various other reasons. Family alone cannot provide that awareness of relationship which was done in the past. Now the school has to provide what home and community provided in the past. "It has to provide total education—education for knowledge, for background, for standards, for awareness, for skills, for understanding, for culture, for making a contribution, for a sense of belonging, for attitudes and for a proper orientation to the modern world."

5. Training of Practical Attitudes and Skills. Happold has rightly said, "Much of the literature, our students read, much of history and geography they learn, they will soon forget, what of value will remain? The ability to read with sense, the ability to speak and write sensitively and precisely, the ability to collect, sift and arrange various sorts of material, the ability to use books as a source both of information and of aesthetic pleasure, and the habit to think clearly and logically, in short, the acquisition of certain tools of learning and of certain skills are essential for every child today." The unified course of Social Studies, through its content and methods, can alone emphasize and train for such attitudes and skills.

6. Need of Enlightened Citizenship. A more enlightened citizenship is the crying need of today. Our schools are called upon to build up a wide-spread interest in current affairs in pupils. It is not possible to give this knowledge only by means of isolated subjects. The content of today teaching must reflect current thought. It must be integrated with actual problems of everyday life. This can be done by the unified course of Social Studies and not by separate subjects like history or geography.

7. Foundation of Later Specialisation. Only a unified course of Social Studies, at the secondary school stage can make specialisation in different subjects easy, at a later stage. It serves as a sure foundation on which the super-structure of specialisation can be built. Therefore, composite course of Social Studies, at secondary school stage, is more useful than separate teaching of history, geography, civics and economics.

Fundamental Postulates for Social Studies Course

1. ***Inter-disciplinary.*** As an inter-disciplinary course it draws its contents selectively from several other branches of knowledge and human experience.
2. ***Applied.*** Social Studies is the applied form of Social sciences, placed in school curriculum to develop proper attitudes, sensibilities and skills among future citizens.
3. ***Pragmatic Approach.*** The approach of Social Studies in teaching is based on a pragmatic philosophy to serve the present needs of a particular society and to help pupils to have social adjustment in their future lives.
4. ***Field.*** The field of Social Studies covers the study of communities at all levels-local, regional, national and international, focusing on man and his social environment.
5. ***Scope.*** The scope of Social Studies is continuously growing, as the social process and problems are changing from time to time. Its content must be revised periodically.
6. ***Emphasis.*** The emphasis of Social Studies lies more on the contemporary human life and its problems than on the past history of man.
7. ***Materials.*** The materials of Social Studies are useful as a media for general education at school level so that pupils may learn them with sufficient ease and interest.

Social Studies provides situations in which school children may use related learnings in a functional and natural setting for the application and use of knowledge and basic skills in solving human problems. Thus, it may be used as a means of integrating various school activities and experiences.

The breadth, comprehensiveness, variety and extension of learning experiences, provided through the teaching of Social Studies, make its scope as wide as the world and as long as the history of man on this earth.

1. ***Study of Human Relationship.*** Human relationships form the nucleus of social studies. These relationships may be studied under four main heads; *(i)* People and People, *(ii)* People and Institutions, *(iii)* People and Earth, and *(iv)* People and Goods. Thus, Social Studies includes the study of those social sciences and humanities which can be applied for a practical understanding of human relationships. These are history, geography, economics, civics, sociology, literature, religion and psychology. But Social Studies views these social sciences as a compact whole. Their limitations are the process of synthesising these subjects into a new field, blending them together, making it a compact and coordinated whole removes. While humanities tend to make man, a man or humanize him.
2. ***Functional Study of Fine Arts.*** Instructional programme of Social Studies also includes the functional study of fine arts like drawing, constructing, painting, music, dance and dramatization. These provide the content needed for a better understanding of people and the world. The functional approach of studies means that whatever factual material is obtained from various fields, should have immediate relationship to the needs and interests of children. Social Studies includes something happening to pupils and teachers and not merely something studied by them.
3. ***Functional Study of Natural Sciences.*** Social sciences and natural sciences are inter-related. Recent advances in the fields of physical sciences, industry and technology have revolutionised social life in all parts of the world. These have extended men's vision from family to neighbourhood, from neighbourhood to town, from town to region, from region to nation and even beyond expanding the area of human relationship from local, regional and

national level to international level. Therefore, the functional study of natural and physical sciences like physics, chemistry, botany, zoology and physiology etc. is an important part of social studies programme.

4. ***Study of Current Affairs.*** Current affairs include those events which deal with the present problems and issues. As every current affair finds its background in the past it provides a great source of both historical and geographical learning. As important elements of social studies current affairs make our historical and social learning concrete. They make us think about the social structure of the community and the effects of social forces in their making.

5. ***Practical Study of Different Resources.*** The Social Studies instructional programme also includes new elements like character education, civil rights, co-operatives, social behaviour, inter-cultural relations and planning. For this purpose, Social Studies must provide excursions and visits to different towns and places of historical, economic, geographical, cultural, scientific and educational importance, utilization of library and community resources, art, and social service activities, debates and dramatization etc. Thus, the field of Social Studies includes the period prior to recorded history and also the foreseeable future. It draws its material from all social sciences and related disciplines as well as from literature, physical sciences, fine arts and religion.

6. ***International Understanding.*** Social Studies seek to promote international understanding of man. Narrow sectional, communal, religious and national claims should be discouraged. Its special purpose in Indian schools to spread a clear understanding of democracy and to secure the whole-hearted acceptance of the values on which it is based. Through a unified course of Social Studies Indian children must learn "Brotherhood of mankind". Even individual has to act, react and interact in a social group,

under social pressure and according to social practices. Therefore, a child must be made familiar with his own needs, the needs of his society and the part he is expected to play. He must be familiar with the significant problems of living together in the modern world.

Thus, Social Studies provides a wide range of materials involved many skills and leading to generalisations. In the words of Ohicholson and Wright "Its scope is really very wide and its theme is the present social life of man, the world over." But Social Studies course is not a limitless and fathomless ocean. It provides only an over-all integrated outline of essential common knowledge so it draws only the functional knowledge from various subjects avoiding the material which has no-bearing on social context. Its subject-matter consists only of very simple and reorganised items of information and experience from various fields having a practical value in the daily lives of children.

EDUCATIONAL FUNCTIONS OF SOCIAL STUDIES

These are as under:

1. ***Introductory Function.*** To acquaint and introduce the children to the physical and social environment and the social and cultural life of the community.
2. ***Instruction Function.*** To acquaint the children with the historic background of mankind, evolution problems and progress of society.
3. ***Cultural Function.*** To create in pupils, interest in the culture of the community to acquire and enrich the cultural heritage.
4. ***Humanitarian Function.*** To throw light and develop understanding on human values of the past, present and future.
5. ***Appreciational Function.*** To develop in them desirable social attitudes such as respect for cultural similarities and dissimilarities and, to appreciate others views, to have tolerance for the mode of living of other people.

6. ***Democratic Function.*** To develop among children understanding of democratic ideals and processes and also insight into democratic ideas and functional aspect.

BASIC GENERAL IDEAS OF SOCIAL STUDIES

For the development of the subject matter and to organise activities, Social Studies takes basic general ideas and concepts from different Social Sciences. The following are the details of generalisations adopted from each social science.

(A) Anthropology. The following generalisation have been adopted from it by Social Studies:

(i) Beliefs, traditions and mode of living of the pre-historic-times can be closely linked with modern immediate environmental conditions.

(ii) Group life originated from family and it become complicated owing to cultural and other changes.

(iii) Modern society is culturally indebted to various aged institutions.

(iv) There is long long impact on man of that culture, in which he is born and brought up.

(v) Culture involves development of knowledge, skill and values developed by human groups.

(B) History. The following generalisations have been adopted from history:

(i) Space and time account for the creation of such a structure in which events occur.

(ii) History does not repeat itself but the events of the past affect those in the present.

(iii) Various inspirers, inspirations and thoughts, may be true or false from historical point and human progress but affect activities at local, national and international levels.

(iv) Mutual dependence plays an important role in determining human relations at each place.

(C) Geography. Following generalisations have been adopted from geography:

(i) The nature, shape and movements of the earth affect all beings who live on it.

(ii) The eliminate is determined by roles of sunlight, temperature, atmospheric pressure, winds, oceanic waves, and mountains.

(iii) Man does labour to meet his need for food, clothing and shelter. For this, he uses and damages the earth.

(iv) The use of natural resources by man is related to his needs and technology.

(v) Land, water and air are natural resources which are absolutely necessary for man.

(D) Economics. The following generalisations have been adopted from economics:

(i) Since wants are unlimited and resources are limited, every nation must tackle the following economic problems:

(a) What comodity to be produced?

(b) How to produce that commodity?

(c) What quantity of it is to be produced?

(d) How to distribute it?

(ii) Labour, natural resources, capital and technology are important factors of production.

(iii) Higher standard of living depends upon productivity.

(E) Sociology. The following ideas and concepts have been accepted from sociology:

(i) Functions in the society are carried by organised groups which are set in the interest of social welfare.

(ii) The goals, beliefs, knowledge and values e transmitted and changed through the agencies of the family, church, school, government and professional institutions.

(iii) For collective activities and cultural advancement, give and take amongst members of the groups is necessary.

(iv) For the existence of society, social control system is a must.

(F) Political Science. The following ideas and concepts have been adopted from political science:

(i) Most of human wants are met in the family, church, press and individual profession, yet the government is an important institution to serve the society.

(ii) The ultimate responsibilities of the government can be categorised under live heads:

(a) External security.

(b) Internal organisation.

(c) Justice.

(d) Compulsory Services for common good.

(e) To offer freedom is a democratic state.

(iii) In ademocracy, the government is the servant of the people, but not vice versa.

(iv) No government can successfully function unless and until it moulds itself to new situations.

(v) For economic, social, cultural and political life, every nation in the world, is a part and parcel of international dependence for organisational purposes.

(G) Philosophy. The following concepts have been accepted from philosophy:

(i) Logic, scientific and ethical analysis are offered by philosophy,

(ii) A free society, keeps research open in its own interest and creates in citizens, habits of conducting research. Social studies, having accepted the above generalisations from social sciences, creates its own integrated and balanced nature *e.g.* In social studies programmes, basic needs,

conduct, culture, values, norms, environment, democracy, comment events etc. are included.

(H) Psychology. The following ideas and concepts are accepted from psychology:

(i) Behaviour is the product of varied, complex and inter related causes.

(ii) Human conduct is the fruit of hereditary and environmental factors.

(iii) Persons differ from each other in respect of personal values, attitudes and personality traits.

(iv) Members of the group subscribe to some general values and characteristics.

(v) Every group affects the conduct of its member.

NEED OF SOCIAL STUDIES IN INDIA

The Indian society of today is quite different from that of yesterday. Changes have occurred in its size and shape and complexion. These social changes have exhibited the need for social ideas. The question itself arises as to what these changes are which have brought for it revolutionary changes, Those changes are presented as under:

1. ***Democratic Government.*** India got freedom after slavery for centuries. The fifteenth August became a Independence Day and simultaneously brought many problems and responsibilities in its wake. We thought that day we have become dutiful having woken up from slumber of ages. We got rights—all civic rights, fundamental rights, political, social and religious and we learnt the lessons of equality, freedom and fraternity. The next step taken was towards democracy and on the 26th Jan. 1950, we declared the nation as a Democratic Republic. This development put heavy responsibilities on, Indians. To make it meaningful and inspiring it became necessary that all people of the nation become efficient citizens, who may successfully run the democratic government and do full justice to rights

and duties granted by the Constitution. For the success in this direction, it is necessary to give to pupils, such education as to make them good citizens and be established in the present democratic society. This aim can be fulfilled with teaching of Social Studies. As we have earlier noted, such a base can be provided through the syllabus of Social Studies and with which we can fully explain the present world to the pupils.

2. ***Socialistic State.*** The important change which occurred in the Indian society is to establish socialistic society and took necessary steps for the same. In the Western countries it was got through violent revolutionary efforts. But the Indian society pursued peaceful steps. In order to evolve it, Sarvodaya, Bhoodan and other non-violent movements were launched. Our late Prime Minister, Jawaharlal Nehru said, "I have faith in socialistic state and education should endeavour to realise it. In case education wants to realise this goal, it will have to include in its curriculum such contents, as would develop in pupile qualities like, social efficiency, cooperation, socially, social justice etc. Social Studies is very much useful in achieving this goal. The main aim of teaching Social Studies is to develop social character. The above account makes it clear that in view of changes in Indian society, it is necessary to teach Social Studies to develop the qualities of democratic citizenship. To fulfil this need it is assigned a place in the educational curriculum.

3. ***Sarvodaya and Establishment of Gram Panchayats.*** Vinoba Bhave, by starting Sarvodaya Movement, endeavoured to initiate great changes in Indian society. The chief aim of this movement was to uplift all people of the society. All people, irrespective of religions and castes should be given equal opportunities for development. Mahatma Gandhi said that for the progress and development of the nation, it is necessary that villages make progress.

He said let the villages be self-governed and self-reliant. On the progress of villages, rests the progress of the nation, since 70% of population, in our country, lives in rural areas. Their standard of living be raised. Let every village be self-governed and self sufficient. For their progress, he emphasised the development of cottage industries, agricultural progress and the establishment of village panchayats. Indian society took important measure to work, according to the teachings of this social reformer, a great teacher and the father of the nation. Owing to this, great changes appeared in the family and village environment. Due to these changes, it came to be felt necessary, to give to citizens such a type of education so that they would, adjust themselves in the environment and understand clearly and in simple form the complexities of human relationships and the social environment. To fulfil this need, the teaching of social studies came to be understood as important and because of this, human relationships and social environment can be given clarity.

4. ***Industrial Progress and the Impact of Scientific Inventions.*** Ours is an agricultural country. After independence, the leaders of the nation, put emphasis on the use of the natural resources for the progress of the nation. This led to the development of several industries in the country. Factories and mills were started. It accounted for a rise in production in the country and which affected the mode of living of the people. Needs of the people multiplied owing to which complexities grew up in their human relationships. Science led to cyclic changes in the structure of the society, complexities cropped now when in the past, the nature of the society was simple. Scientists led rural atmosphere to international environment. Owing to these inventions the world of today, has shrunk very much. The rural life also was affected by these inventions. Now power, tubewell, new manures, new tools are being used in villages. The villager of today cannot remain contented with his

environment, but it is needed for him to know about international environment. Competition amongst scientists may lead to destruction of the world. History bears testimony to the two world wars witnessed, and on account of this competition, and is heading towards the third. If humanity is to be saved from destruction, the knowledge of Social Studies is essential so that he may get knowledge about human relationships and their involvement. To fulfil this need, every country is assigning to social studies, an important place in its educational set-up. For the same reason India has also given an important place to social studies, in the curriculum. There is another reason also that India has been, diffusing the message of universal brotherhood ever since.

IMPORTANCE OF SOCIAL STUDIES/SOCIAL SCIENCE

We can study this under two heads:

1. **In its Individual Context.** From this point, this study has importance as follows:
   - *(a)* ***Building Social Character.*** This accounts for developing several social qualities like cooperation, sympathy, impartiality etc. The qualities work as the basis for building social character.
   - *(b)* To develop the various mental faculties of the individual.
   - *(c)* To prepare the individual for evolving practical solutions of problems.
   - *(d)* To enable an individual to discharge his responsibilities.
   - *(e)* To develop various social habits and skills.
   - *(f)* To enable him to adjust himself in the environment. In addition, he is enabled to adjust suitably to his needs.
2. **In Social Context.** In the present social conditions, the importance of social studies has increased owing to the following reasons:

(a) It helps in developing healthy outlook in pupils.

(b) It develops the spirit of cooperation among citizens.

(c) It awakens love and respect and faith in the national heritage and culture.

(d) It prepares the way for the progress of society.

(e) Helps in bringing about integration and stability in the society.

(f) It is highly useful in making social life progressive, successful and prosperous.

(g) Helps in developing awareness and international understanding in the society.

(h) It develops tolerance, sympathy and love for fellow beings.

(i) It helps in developing liberal outlook by counteracting prejudices and bias.

(j) Helps in leading life by promoting critical thinking.

❑

2

Aims and Methods of Social Studies

So far we have discussed the concept of Social Studies. Now, we must, for our guidance and clear understanding, know what the aims of teaching Social Studies are. These are in turn determined by the general aims of education. Education has three aims: *(a)* Cultural *(b)* Individual and *(c)* Social. One thing as regards Social Studies is clear that it aims at socialising the child. This is the outcome of the new democratic and social approach is education.

Bining and Bining give the following aims of social studies.

A. General Aims

B. Specific Aims

A. GENERAL AIMS

1. Enrichment and development of the mind of the child to the greatest possible extent through environments.
2. To train the pupils to prepare themselves for the democratic society. Knowledge of mere facts cannot suffice, we must introduce practical activities for the accomplishment of these aims. Inculcation of sympathy for the mankind, tolerance, constructive thinking and hard labour should be the real purpose.

B. SPECIFIC AIMS

1. To combine the material of history, geography, civics and material from other fields into a single integrated course. Through this course, the child comes to understand the interdependence of different environments.
2. To help in the co-ordination of the curriculum as a whole. Social Studies forms the core of the entire scheme of teaching.
3. It causes social awakening and creates a sense of duty and responsibility.
4. To offer opportunities for self-development and personal achievement.
5. To foster worthwhile attitude towards knowledge and life.
6. To cause an experience of study that will promote continuation of education throughout life.
7. To provide for clear thinking, flexibility of mind, sound standards of action and cosmopolitanism.

Mr. Wesly gives a clear idea of the aims of Social Studies in his book. *"Teaching of Social Studies in High Schools"*.

1. To acquire social concept.
2. To develop study and reading skills.
3. Development of good personality.
4. To enable them to assume responsibility.
5. To prepare them for useful work.
6. Formation of good traits.
7. To learn the technique of co-operation.
8. To understand the interdependence of people.
9. To make them thoughtful consumers.
10. To enable them to become participating citizens.
11. To uphold democracy.

12. To promote world peace.
13. To develop political thinking.
14. To teach them to respect all religions, races and groups.

AIMS OF TEACHING SOCIAL STUDIES

1. To develop a broad human interest in the progress of mankind in general and India in particular.
2. To develop in the pupils a proper understanding of their social and geographical environments and to awaken the urge to improve it.
3. To develop a sense of rights and responsibilities of citizenship.
4. To develop the individual and social virtues which make a man reliable associate and trusted neighbour.
5. To inculcate the love for the motherland, reverence for its past and a belief in its failure, as the home of a united, cooperative society based on love, truth and justice.
6. To present to the child biographical sketches of great men of the world to enable him to imbibe ideals of character.
7. To develop mutual respect for all religions.
8. To help the child in developing his sense of self-respect and responsibility.
9. To build in him habits of personal cleanlines and awaken in him a sense of keeping his surrounding clean.

The following are important Aims of Teaching Social Studies:

1. Enrichment and Development of the Lives of Pupils in their Environment. One most important aim of Social Studies is to help the pupils to understand the environment in which they live; how it influences the individual and the community and how the individual and the community collectively influence it. Students must appreciate the inter-relationship of the elements of their environment through the integrated subject-matter from history, geography, civics, economics and sociology. They must know the past and the present struggles of mankind and think of making their own personal contribution towards future progress. Development of institutions of the past such as state, church and business concerns, school etc, and the changes they have undergone to meet the demands of changing times, must also be known to children.

2. Acquisition of Knowledge. A certain amount of definite knowledge is essential for good citizenship. This contributes directly to social progress because exact knowledge is necessary for clear thinking and reservation of judgement. Factual knowledge also satisfies the natural curiosity of pupils quickens their imagination and helps them in building up individual interests. Without clear thinking and critical Judgement many problems of modern civilization cannot be solved. Factual knowledge is also the basis of sympathy and understanding which are so essential for social intercourse and social solidarity. Definite knowledge of Social Studies promotes understanding of all history and all human experiences as a process of change and development. It also makes clear to pupils that social changes are inevitable as a result of scientific advancement and that individualism should give place to collectivism.

3. Development of Right Attitudes. Development of right attitude is also one of the major aims of teaching Social Studies. Desirable attitudes are essential because they are extremely significant factor of behaviour. They are based on an appreciation of things which are worthwhile in life. Attitudes depend upon intellectual and emotional factors.

Scientific attitude is intellectual because in it judgements are based on facts, unaffected by personal feelings. Emotional attitude on the other hand, includes prejudice, jealousy, bad temper, disobedience, laziness, etc. Most of these attitudes whether good or bad, are combination of intellectual and emotional feelings. The teacher's duty; therefore, is to help the pupils in building up the right attitudes. But before doing so, the teacher himself, at all times must-exhibit self-control, patience, sympathy and self-respect, if he wishes to secure good and favourable results. He will thus, be able to develop desirable attitudes among his pupils by his own example.

4. Training on Desirable Pattern of Conduct. There was a time when home and society participated in the educational process of children. But now both home and society have ceased to play their important role in the development of character and behaviour of children to the desired extent. Their duty and function are to be performed in school. Thus the entire burden of training children in the right type of behaviour and conduct is to be borne by the school. It is, therefore, the duty of the school to develop desirable pattern of conduct among children and thus help in the building up of character in order to produce good citizens. And the Social Studies teacher is in an excellent position to inculcate all this by virtue of the subject-matter that he teaches and the methods that he follows. Through content and teaching procedures, schools can educate the pupils in competent citizenship. For affecting a change in the human sector, training in the right lines must be given in the formative period of life.

5. Formation of Habits and Skills. In social studies, habits and skills form an important part of the work. Habit is a simple acquired tendency to act. In social studies we aim at developing habits not only of accuracy, speed, neatness and independent study but a very wide range of them, from the habit of using references and text books intelligently to the habit of controlling one's emotions under extreme provocation.

A skill is a complex of simple habits used with greater consciousness of the end in view. In Social Studies skills as the making of outlines; maps, charts, graphs and models should constitute an important part of the instructional work.

6. Socialisation of Pupils. Another important aim of teaching Social Studies is the socialisation of pupils in order to make them well-informed and enlightened citizens, capable of promoting common welfare. Socialisation will awaken in them a sense which develop confidence, courage and happiness. It will all of individual and social virtues of initiative, truthfulness, righteousness, constructive thinking, critical judgement, just, tolerance, cooperation, fellow-feeling and sacrifice, etc, for making a person a reliable associate and a trusted neighbour. Teacher should begin to appreciate India's rich cultural heritage.

7. Development of a Sense of Belongingness. One of our important aim of teaching Social Studies is to develop among our students a sense of belongingness—belonging to a place, to a community, to a nation and to the world. Thus, we should give detailed information about man's multifarious relationship. This will create in our students a realisation of interdependence of man and man, nation and nation and thus help in promoting international understanding and respect for humanity. It will also promote mutual respect for religious institutions, and modes and ways of life of different peoples of world, to understand each other fully and to know each others problems and their solutions.

It is thus quite clear from the aims and objectives, mentioned in the foregoing pages that a good and useful individual life, an ideal society and a perfect state well emerge if Social Studies is taught with these aims in view. At this stage to relate ideas to meaningful concept and then to make generalisations.

DIFFERENCE BETWEEN AIMS AND VALUES

Education is a purposeful process. So, it cannot be thought of in the absence of aims. In other words, it can be said that education has some aim or another. While fullfiling these aims, many experiences are got. These earned experiences or outcomes are known as 'Values'. In the course of our quest aims continue to remain there before us. Our aim can be one, button the course of our efforts to obtain it, we get several experiences which become values. It is not necessary that we may always attain aims. Sometimes, while achieving the aims we get many experiences. Such obtained experiences or outcomes, fall in the category of values. With these values and experiences whatever desirable changes are brought about in the behaviour of the child, are kept in the category of attainable aims. In brief the difference between the two can be explained as under:

Aims	Values
1. They are idealistic which can not be fully achieved.	1. These are realistic and are achievable.
2. By nature those are general, philosophical and theoretical.	2. These are by nature practical and specific.
3. These are set before teaching and learning commences.	3. These emerge in the course of learning and teaching.
4. These are desirable goals.	4. These are the probable outcomes of aims.

VALUES OF TEACHING SOCIAL STUDIES

While teaching social studies effectively we achieve several values. Chief out of these are discussed below:

1. ***Development of Social Qualities.*** The study of this subject develops civic qualities, beneficial for the society which are necessary for the success of democracy.
2. ***Development of Desirable Attitudes.*** The pupils through the study of this subject develop desirable social skills and attitudes to discharge social function and civic responsibilities. This develops ability to work according to democratic principles. It develops healthy feelings and proper and logical decision-taking attitudes.
3. ***Knowledge with Experience.*** Along with knowledge, experience is also acquired. Decisions are taken about situations by learning through activities. Pupils are not given only bookish knowledge. They do not comprehend the real facts only. Realistic situations are created so that the child gets knowledge through activities and experiences. He will take more interest in the lesson and the teacher will get full cooperation.
4. ***Training in Cooperation.*** Whether in school or community individualistic outlook is seen. In schools pupils do not carry out activities, in cooperation, and in the community

every person thinks of his own benefit. But this outlook is very dangerous in modem times. So, through Social Studies training is given to pupils to work in cooperation in and outside class.

5. ***Development of Good Habits.*** It develops good habits in pupils; good qualities like cooperation, brotherliness etc., develop in them.
6. ***Development of Spirit of Adjustment.*** It develops in pupils the spirit of adjustment with modern conditions, by explaining to them the complexities of the society.
7. ***To Develop New Relationship between Teacher and Taught.*** Since achievements are made through activities, there comes into being a new type of relationship between the teacher and taught. They plan to wode together. Activities are organised in an informal manner in which pupils are given every type of freedom to have exchange of ideas, without obstacles.
8. ***Development of International Understanding.*** With the study of this subject, international understanding and world brotherhood feelings develop.
9. ***Helps Slow Learners and Backward Children.*** This subject can help the slow learners and backward children. Generally it is seen that narrow knowledge given to pupils in traditional ways, they fail to assimilate. To such pupils also this subject offers adequate opportunities for cooperation under different situations.
10. ***Intellectual Development.*** Pupils themselves collect material for study and it develops their mind. Pupils do not get ready made answers to questions but they are encouraged to concentrate on new problems with a view, to work out solution.

MEANING OF TEACHING METHOD

It is a means which the teacher adopts in order to make learning simple.

There are two view points about teaching method. According to one every teacher should have knowledge of various teaching methods. The second view point is that if the teacher has full knowledge of the subject-matter, then he need not know or use any method. Here, the first view point gives a great importance to teaching methods. Really speaking both the view points are defective. For successful teaching the teacher should have adequate knowledge of both *i.e.*, the subject-matter and teaching methods. With the reconciliation of the two only; success of teaching will be possible.

Binning & Binning, "If teaching is to reach its highest degree of efficiency, it is evident that teachers must be thoroughly trained in material instruction in their fields and must also possess a broad understanding of all phases of method—including psychology—as a part of that philosophy of education which is essential to good teaching."

The term, 'Method' in education is used to refer to those processes of the teacher, through which the pupil learns the knowledge of the subject-matter. The importance of the teaching method in respect of a subject is similar to the right path leading to the set destination.

According to John Dewey, "Method is a way of managing to develop conclusion."

According to E.B. Wesley, "Method of teaching in education refers to the series of activities for guidance adopted by the teacher, which transform into learning on the part of the pupils."

So, the method is not an activity, but is a process which does not confine to anyone step, but is created by linking many steps and their balanced form gives rise to a method.

IMPORTANCE OF TEACHING METHOD

It is necessary for the teacher to have knowledge of right methods.

The Secondary Education Commission 1952, writes in the report, "Even the best curriculum and the most perfect syllabus remains dead unless quickened into life by the right methods of teaching and the right kind of teachers."

Mrs. S.K. Kochhar, in her book, *'Method and Technique of Teaching'* has beautifully interpreted the importance of teaching methods. She writes, "A teacher must be fully conversant with the different methods of teaching in the same way as a soldier is to be conversant with the various weapons of fighting. Which methods he should use at a particular time depends upon his judgement."

Thus the teaching methods are very important in the teaching-learning process. Teaching methods make teaching systematic and simple. It is necessary for all teachers to have the knowledge of teaching methods. Teaching methods are closely related with the aims and values of education and help in achieving them.

Teaching methods are very important in teaching work, but the teacher should use them very carefully. To drag all, with the same staff is improper. In the same way it is equally unsuitable to teach all subjects or to teach all pupils with one and the same method. The teacher should alter methods in accordance with subject-matter, the needs and aptitudes of pupils. In education, the teaching method should not be confined to a certain stable aspect.

According to Binning & Binning, "Methodology should be conceived as a dynamic function of education and not as a static aspect of the process of teaching."

At the same time while using teaching methods, the teacher should keep in mind his own aptitudes and abilities. He should see that he possesses such aptitudes and abilities which enable him to use a modem method. The teacher should make the method his servant. If a method does not work successfully owing to particular reasons, then the teacher should abandon that method and should adopt any other method. For this the teacher should know all teaching methods.

In the words of Binning & Binning, "The successful teacher is he who them is familiar with all the methods and who them, with his aims clearly in view selects the method that will best aid him in attaining them."

The above account makes it clear that to teach a subject-matter successfully, teaching methods are very important and these methods are closely related to aims and values of education.

CHARACTERISTICS OF GOOD METHOD

Good methods used in teaching, have the following characteristics:

1. These are helpful in achieving pre-determined aims and objectives.
2. The method should be defmite and suitable for that particular topic and class.
3. A method should be such as to inspire pupils for activity and self study.
4. A method should be such as to make pupils active participants in the teaching learning process.
5. A good method is practical. It enables the teacher to know what is desirable and what is not.
6. A good method is dynamic.

   The method should include adequate activities so as to enable pupils for self expression.
7. A good method develops in pupils, reasoning, decision making, analytical faculty and fully takes cognisance of individual differences.

On the basis of above stated features, the teacher plays the role of a guide. The subject-matter and teaching method should be determined from the point of view of the pupil.

METHOD OF TEACHING SOCIAL STUDIES

After selecting the subject-matter, it becomes the duty of the teacher to see how it may be taught and learnt. This can be possible only by using effective methods. There are two main types of methods.

QUESTION-ANSWER METHOD

In Question-Answer method of teaching social studies the teacher puts the questions to the pupils while the answers given by the pupils are supplemented and elaborated by him. In asking questions, the relevant experiences in the memory of the students come to the surface and the familiar and known association help in learning and granting the unfamiliar and the unknown. The pupils readjust the old for acquiring new knowledge. As the old and the new get integrated the process of learning social studies becomes simpler and easier.

In this method the teacher puts questions to the pupils to motivate them and create a felt need for learning something new or solve some new problems. In the beginning questions are asked directly about such past experiences of the pupils which are relevant to the present lesson. They are put in a manner that the present topic appears to the pupils as a problem in whose solution they may be naturally interested. These are generally developmental questions both the narrative and developmental questions are used in the presentation stage. It seeks the solution to the problem developed during the preparation or introduction stage. In the recapitulation or application stage, questions are asked to find out the grasp of the subject-matter or to help the pupils apply the knowledge granted to new situations. Thus, learning is consolidated and insight deepened.

Advantages. The question-answer procedure develops the pupil's insight into the lesson. It leads to the understanding and comprehension of the subject-matter presented.

The question-answer method ensures active participation of the pupils.

Supported by different visual aids like pictures, charts, films, filmstrips, etc., and devices like dramatization in different forms this method can go a long way in sustaining the interest of the pupils.

OBSERVATION METHOD

Importance. Immediate surroundings and community afford many opportunities for observation. Concrete tangible, visible and describable data on cultural, industrial, political and geographic facts and relationships prove invaluable for the teaching of social studies. Observation lends vitality to the subject-matter of social studies. Direct experiences are more effective in the process of learning they are also retained for a longer period of time. As rich, full-bodied purposeful experiences seen, handled, tasted, touched, felt and smelled. They are the unabridged version of life itself. A trip to a monument, a fort, a temple, an institution, provides its first-hand experiences which are real. The children can see them, ask questions about them and examine them. Such experiences are highly conducive to learning.

Advantages. Under the careful guidance of social studies teacher's observation provides the pupils ample opportunities for asking questions, gathering data and .pooling information. Visit to telephone exchanges, newspaper and telegraph offices clarify ideas about communication. Study trips to airports and other transportation centres show how people and goods are moved about. Production and consumption can be understood better when pupils see the stores, the markets and factories of the community.

Techniques of Observation

1. ***Field Trips.*** Field trips are undertaken for securing information, changing attitudes, awakening interests, developing appreciation, promoting ideas and enjoying new experiences. Used to initiate a unit of study; they may be a part of its core and they can give it the final touch.

2. ***Community Service Projects.*** Community service projects involve individual activity of an integrated, mental, physical, emotional and spiritual nature. They are of genuine educational value to the pupil as well as to the society.

3. ***Community Surveys.*** Community surveys foster comprehensive understanding of community structure and processes in their everyday operation, interaction and complexity. In stimulating depth of insight into vital community problems and trends which have been influenced by past conditions, present developments and future prospects community surveys are very useful.

There can be no difficulty in preparing a catalogue of the available resources for proper and detailed study if the teacher is resourceful and the class is enthusiastic and clever. The resources which need to be observed by the pupils vary from community to community. There may be classified under various heads such as resources of geographical, historical, cultural, economic and scientific interests. For the observation of the resources leading maximum benefit to the pupils proper procedure should be followed.

CONVERSATIONAL METHOD

This method follows the question-answer technique. While the teacher puts the questions to the pupils, the answers given by the latter lead to the development of the lesson. The teacher supplements and elaborates the answers of the pupils from time to time. By asking questions, the relevant past experiences come to the fore. The familiar and known association help in learning and grasping the unfamiliar and unknown. The pupils readjust the old and the new to integrate it and to simply the process of learning social studies.

Procedure

1. *Preparation Stage.* During the preparation stage, questions are asked directly on past experiences of the pupils relevant to the present lesson in a way that the present lesson appears as a problem in whose solution pupils are naturally interested. These questions are generally developmental.

2. *Application Stage.* In this stage questions are asked to help pupils apply the knowledge gained to new situations to consolidate and deepen insight.

3. *Presentation Stage.* In the presentation stage, both the narrative and developmental questions are used to solve the problem developed during the preparation stage. This procedure develops pupils insight into the lesson. It leads to the learning of the subject-matter presented.

Advantages. The conversational method or Question-Answer method is a good method of teaching social studies. It should be supported by visual aids like pictures, charts, models, films, filmstrips and devices like dramatization in different forms. Thus, this ensures interest of the pupils and learning becomes an interesting experience.

Reasons for Use

1. *Unsuitable Text-books.* One of the reasons for the use of this method by most of our social studies teachers is the absence of suitable text-books. In text-books, while some topics are magnified beyond proportion as they have some individual appeal for the author, other topics receive only scanty treatment. The language of most of the text-books is tough. As the text-books meant for school children are written by university and college professors neither having experience of teaching youngsters nor being conversant with their psychological needs, the reading material is tough and beyond the comprehension of average students. These teachers start dictating notes to get speedy results.

2. *Shortage of Time.* As the curriculum in social studies is overcrowded the social studies teacher looks for a short-cut-dictation of notes to finish the course in time.

3. *Needed for Examination.* Teachers dictate notes of important and expected questions to get good results in examinations.

4. *Fatigue.* In our schools a social studies teacher is generally overburdened with work. As he is expected to take more than thirty periods in a week he does not get enough time for preparation. If he is allotted some period towards the fag-end of the day most of the pupils are already tired due to strenuous work put in the preceding periods, in such exacting subjects as Mathematics, English etc. To keep them engaged and to avoid the distraction or attention on the part of students due to exhaustion the teacher starts dictating notes.

5. *Teachers Lacking Power of Expression.* Social studies teachers which lack the power of expression can neither narrate nor lecture well. Therefore, they resort to note-dictation saving the trouble of making preparation for narration or lecture.

Style of Notes Dictation

1. *Notes on Important Topic Only.* Some teachers give detailed notes on important topics only such as cold war, technological development, international peace, and cooperation, new economic order, Fascism and Nazism etc. As a normal practice, these notes are given, when the teacher has already discussed the topics in the class.

2. ***Substance on Blackboard.*** After explaining the topic in detail some teachers give notes in the form of substance on the black-board.

They also require the pupils to prepare the lesson at home in advance. They are asked only to copy the substance from the black-board.

3. ***Question-Answer.*** Teachers who give notes in the question-answer from select important and expected questions and dictate answers.

Disadvantages of Dictating Notes

1. ***No use of Critical Power.*** Note dictated obstruct the use of critical powers, which is one of the important aims of teaching social studies. Taking the matter dictated by the teacher as gospel truth a pupil crams it without testing the relevance of the material.

2. ***No Insight in the Subject.*** Pupils fail to develop the habit of consulting reference books; Disregarding the text-books they fail to develop proper insight into the subject.

3. ***Based on the False Principle.*** It is based on the false principle that instruction is a process of memorisation. This social studies teaching is made synonymous with the memorisation of facts communicated by the teacher.

Thus, the pupils should think and express, consult all possible good works on the subject and prepare their own notes in social studies.

DISCUSSION METHOD

One of the most valuable methods of teaching social studies is discussion. It is said, "two heads are better than one". Wonderful results are achieved when a number of heads combine to solve a problem.

Advantages

1. This method is best for a problem, an issue or a situation in which there a difference of opinion. In the discussion method of teaching social studies there is exchange of opinion accompanied by a search for its factual basis.
2. Speech is free and responsible. Values are created not quarrelled about. The participants are engaged in a process of competitive cooperation. Agreement is the declared purpose of discussion which is an ordered process of collective decision-making.
3. If agreement is not reached, discussion has the value of clarifying and sharpening the nature of agreement.

Objectives of Discussion

As a method of teaching social studies discussion may be used for the following objectives:

(i) To lay plans for new work;
(ii) To make decisions concerning future action;
(iii) To obtain and gaining respect for various points of view;
(iv) To clarify ideas;
(v) To share information;
(vi) To inspire interest; and
(vii) To evaluate progress.

Steps in Discussion

1. In the case of problems:
   (i) Locating and defining problems of common interest and significance;
   (ii) Working together to find ways of solving the problems;
   (iii) Evaluating the effectiveness of the suggested solutions and their implementations;
   (iv) Allocating responsibilities for the solutions suggested.

2. In case of plans for projects and programmes:
   (i) Deciding on the programme and the particulars such as date time and place;
   (ii) Enumerating the jobs to be done in organising the programme;
   (iii) Allocating duties to the members of the group; and
   (iv) Evaluating the results.

Forms of Discussion

1. *Debate.* In the programme of debate two or more students holding contradictory opinions present arguments on a particular problem. They also rebut the opposite side. Finally the rest of the class is encouraged to ask questions from the debaters or engage in a brief discussion with them. A debate requires a moderator. The teacher should work both with the debaters and the class in order to get significant results.

Some Topic for Debate

1. Globalisation is necessary for the economic development of India.
2. Capitalism is responsible for the poverty of our country.
3. Five Year Plans have failed to generate proper development.
4. Democracy is the best form of government.
5. For forms of government let fools contest, that which is governed least is best.
6. If Raja Ram Mohan Rai had not started the Reformation Movement in India, the political and economic history of India would have taken a different course.
7. Fundamental rights are of no use in India.
8. User needs total disarmament.
9. Democracy in India is more formal than real.
10. Preventive detention of citizens deprives them of their fundamental rights.

2. *Symposium.* In a symposium the participants present to the audience through speeches or proper reading their views about various aspects of a selected problem or topic. To quote Struck, "We think of a symposium as a group of comments, either spoken or written, which portrays contrasting or at least different points of view". The objective of the symposium is to clarify thoughts upon controversial questions. The audience listens to the discussion. Each person forms his own conclusions concerning the validity of the points of view presented. The ideal number of pupil participants in a symposium is four or five.

3. *Panel Discussions.* It is a discussion among a selected group persons, large enough for variety and small enough for purposeful deliberations. The ideal number may be four to six persons. The participants in a panel discussion are usually eminent persons in their fields. They present various points of view before an audience which subsequently joins in the discussion. The purpose of panel discussion is to get important facts from different angles, to stimulate thinking and lay a basis for wide participation. No speeches are made by the members among them only informal conversations take place.

Rotation System : The rotation system may be followed in a panel discussion. Each member expresses his opinion in turn or the members speak briefly as the thought comes to them one after the other.

Advantages

Panel discussion method provides a natural setting in which people get the opportunity to ask questions, to evaluate replies and to contribute constructively.

4. *Brain Storming.* In this form of discussion the brains of the participants are stimulated to create a storm of ideas and give suggestions regarding the topic without any deliberation to find whether or not they are meaningful and purposeful. When the brain is let go thus without social institutions, it would be able to give expressions to some of the most useful and practical suggestions. For example "Small saving could do a lot to strengthen the savings movement" is a good subject for brain storming.

Procedure of Discussion

1. *Planning.* To make proper use of the discussion method the teacher and student representatives should do considerable planning. In planned and well-directed procedure discussion the whole process may be divided into three stages—preparation, discussion and evaluation.

2. *Preparation.* For through preparation for the discussion the teacher should read wide and deep purposefully and critically and prepare the material conscientiously. Arranged logically points to be discussed should be written on the chalk board for guidance. If the students do not initially feel the need of the problem to be discussed they should be made to do so.

3. *Conducting.* The conducting the discussion should be disciplined. The arrangement of seats should ensure face-to-face talk. The strength of the discussion is obtained from the information and viewpoint of all members of the group. All should contribute to its progress as it is a thinking-together process which breaks-down if one member of the group dominates it. Ensuring that every member to the group participates the teacher should encourage sincere questions and comments. He must gear the discussion to the realization of specific objectives and development of proper skills and methods.

4. *Evaluation.* Discussion results in expanding information or lessening or removing prejudices, changing attitudes or ideals, increasing the range of interest, altering ideas concerning national and international policies, or causing a member to become a more active citizen. One must evaluate the discussion with these motives in mind.

Advantages of Discussion

(i) Useful Both for the Juniors and Seniors. Junior children learn through conversation and discussion, to take turns, listen attentively, act cooperatively, speak distinctly, stand and sit correctly, respect the ideas of others, share interests, ask pertinent questions, utilize simple information and comprehend the problem before the group. Senior children plan and discuss problems with the entire group and in smaller units. The group learns together and presents important information, makes suggestions, shares responsibility, comprehends the topic, evaluates the findings and summarises results.

(ii) Increase in Knowledge. Through discussion children crystallise their thinking and identify concepts needing further study. Therefore, their knowledge of social studies becomes clear.

(iii) Moderation. Through discussion students know and understand that difference in perspective need not result in disaster and that people may believe in the same thing for different reasons.

(iv) Clarification and Sharpening of the Issues. In discussion new ground is discovered both for agreement and disagreement. Old ideas and values may be replaced by new ones.

(v) Knowledge of Limitations. The student discovers what he did not know, what he has overlooked and wherein he was mistaken both as to facts and the method of interpreting them. He may find out what he knows and the surety with which he knows it.

(vi) Knowledge is Given a Round Trip. Discussion is not the oneway affair of the teacher. It engenders more reflection than the question and answer recitation. Of all the methods of teaching social studies discussion is farthest from rote learning. In place of cajolery, threat, coercion or propaganda it employs reasonable persuasion.

(vii) Helpful in Establishing an Attitude of Looking Forward to Progress and Growth. Self-evaluation. Discussion activates thinking along the lines of self-evaluation.

(viii) Discovering Leaders. Discussion helps the teacher in discovering students with a potential for becoming genuine leaders.

(ix) Intellectual Team Work. Discussion represents a type of intellectual team-work resting on the principle that the pooled knowledge, ideas and feelings of several persons have greater merit than those of a single individual.

(x) Tolerance. Discussion engenders toleration for views which are at variance, from those one holds.

ASSIGNMENT METHOD

Assignment method is advocated for the teaching of social studies in higher classes. Where the whole of the syllabus is split into significant topics or units and each topic or unit is sub-divided into assignments. The pupils prepare the assignments in writing. This helps in organisation of knowledge, assimilation of facts and better preparation for examinations.

Types of Assignments

1. ***Preparatory Assignments.*** Through these assignments meant for circulation the pupils can be prepared for the work which is to follow on the next day. This preliminary pilot work enables the teacher to lead the class with ease and understanding.

2. ***Study Assignments.*** These include problem-solving assignments, assignments on making and handling tools, assignments on picture reading, assignments for the preparation of a topic in the light of references provided.

Following are some problem-solving assignments:

- *(i)* ***Solving Problems of a Mathematical Nature.*** With an average speed of 500 miles per hour a jet air-liner is going round the world on a non-stop flight. How many hours will take to complete a flight *(i)* along the tropic of cancer and *(ii)* along the 30 N latitude.
- *(ii)* ***Searching for Causes.*** A traveller resolved to go round the world in 80 days. He reached 5 minutes late and was sorry about it. However, his friends told him that they were surprised to see him reach there a day in advance.
- *(iii)* ***Assignments on Making and Handling Tools.*** These include assignments of taking readings, and maintaining records. Converting recorded data into geographical tools for better and clearer understanding, preparing simple and interesting geographical tools, preparing models and charts, interpreting graphs, charts and cartograms.
- *(iv)* ***Assignments on Picture.*** These include assignments on picture-reading as review revision through pictures,

correlating a picture with a plan, an air view, or a map, matching pictures and places, clarifying concepts through pictures, selecting and appreciating the best pictures, etc.

(v) ***Creative Assignment.*** These include assignments for listing points in favour of, or against a given argument, reaching valid conclusions from statistical or visual data, writing letters, dialogues imaginary travelogues and autobiographical accounts of imaginary situations, etc.

(vi) ***Remedial Assignments.*** Revised in the light of pupil's reactions to the three types of assignments mentioned above, the purpose of these assignments is to remove weak points and clear misunderstandings.

(vii) ***Revisional Assignments.*** Keeping in view the specific objectives of the subject-matter being tested these assignments are worked out in advance. These include assignments for *(a)* providing drill to the work done by the students, and *(b)* for checking their retention and reproduction of facts, incidents, etc., of the topic and *(c)* for checking the understanding of the topic.

Parts of Assignment Lesson

1. ***Preparation.*** In preparation efforts are made for developing the pupils interest in writing the assignment. This work can be completed in one period. Broadheads should be outlined under which the assignment is to be written. The necessary information, including the references, etc. be given which would help the pupils in working out the assignment.

2. ***Writing.*** This work may take more than one class period. The pupils may write the assignment at home or in the class. If they write in assignment in the class under the supervision of the teacher, they should be allowed the facilities to consult books and ask questions whenever necessary.

3. ***Selection of Pairs for Mutual Corrections.*** To help them in correction work the pupils may be given a list of the types of probable errors occurring in writing social studies assignments such as omission of vital facts, wrong statement of facts, statement of irrelevant facts, failure to bring out causal relationships, etc.

4. ***Teachers Work.*** This includes correction of sample assignment scripts by the teacher and preparation of common list of errors.

5. ***Discussion of the List in a Correction Class.*** Finally the common errors committed by the pupils should be discussed in a correction class to check their recurrence.

6. ***Correction by Pupils.*** Now the pupils may be asked to correct their assignments at home.

Advantages of Assignment

1. ***Teachers Knowing the Interests of his Pupils in a Particular Subject-area.*** He is also able to discover the specific abilities of the individual pupil which may be developed and used for their own good.

2. ***Suitability.*** The method is quite suitable for pupils of different ability levels such as gifted, average and slow learners.

3. ***Teachers Foreseeing of the Difficulties which the Students may have to Face in the Learning of the Topic.*** The teacher can guide the pupils by intelligently putting thought-provoking questions in his assignments. The question and guidance to read or to study a topic will prepare the pupils to face the difficulties boldly.

UNIT METHOD

It is a new experiment in education, to teach subject-matter methodically in the form of units.

It is based upon *Gestalt* psychology. According to it our attention is drawn *(i)* to the object in its whole form and *(ii)* we accept one object in place of another. So, the second object becomes the basis for the first one. So after full attention is focussed on the whole object, attention is then given, to its parts. Just as, when a person comes to us, his entire picture is drawn upon and later on attention goes to the different parts of his body.

Thus, with reference to education the pupils attention is readily engaged by the whole form of the subject matter and subsequently to other elements. Hence, the teacher should, in the process of teaching while presenting every topic in a serial order use Unit Method in lesson platting and thereby should make teaching natural and effective.

Different educators have accepted 'Unit Method' as a purposeful organisation of activities which is related to some or another in the first instance the object is presented in the whole form and subsequently relation is established with experiences, activities and conduct. Thus, the Unit Method helps in making teaching process clear, effective and useful.

H.C. Mormon, "Unit is a comprehensive and significant aspect of the environment, of an organised science, of an art, or of conduct which on being learnt results in an adaptation of personality.

According to Thomas M. Risk, "The term 'Unit' signifies the unity or wholeness of learning activities relating to some problems or project."

N.C.E.R.T. "A unit is an instructional device which gives knowledge to students in a composite manner."

G.V. Good. "Unit is a major sub-division of course of study, a text-book or a subject field, particularly a sub-division of Social Studies, practical arts or science also. It is an organisation of various activities, experiences and types of learning around a central theme, problem or purpose, developed cooperatively by a group of pupils-teacher leadership. It involves planning, execution of plan and evaluation of results."

James M.Lee. "A unit is the general content process frame-work for the learning of the various inter-related facts of the topic or problem. Hence a unit is a pattern of organisation, not a method of teaching.

Above definitions are not entirely accepted because no one definition has been evolved so far as may be acceptable to all educators.

STEPS OF UNIT METHOD

Some scholars have made efforts to present unit technique in the form of a teaching method. To make it useful for class teaching. Morrison advocates five steps. Risk advocates three steps in this method. The separate analysis of teaching steps as given by the two scholars is given as under. Risk writes, "The unit plan teaching technique consists simply the following of the major psychological steps in developing a unit. "He gave the following three steps of Unit teaching:

(a) Introducing the units and devices

(b) Developing the unit

(c) Culminating the unit

Morrison advocate the following five steps in unit teaching:

1. ***Exploration.*** In this stage, the teacher ascertains how much previous knowledge the pupils have, relating to the new unit. The teacher can ascertain the previous knowledge of pupils using the following devices and ways:
   (a) Written test,
   (b) Through oral questions, and
   (c) By exchange of views.
2. ***Presentation.*** At this stage the teacher presents the subject-matter through conversation or narration. Subsequently; with the help of questioning he ascertains if the pupils have grasped the subject-matter of the unit. If they have not understood it the teacher will again present the same. He will move to the next step after the pupils have demonstrated that they have understood the unit.
3. ***Organisation.*** In this stage pupils organise knowledge, by systematically writing the subject-matter of the unit. If they succeed in doing so, the teacher takes for granted, that the pupils have thoroughly understood the subject-matter of the unit.

4. ***Assimilation.*** Pupils are give opportunity to digest the subject-matter of the unit. At this stage, the pupils, can assimilate the subject-matter through the following medium:
   (i) By studying
   (ii) By writing
   (iii) By talking to each other, and
   (iv) Consultation with the teacher.

Thus, this method takes the mixed form of 'supervised study' and "laboratory method'.

5. ***Recitation.*** Now the pupils are in a position to recite all or important portions. This step is important for giving training to speak.

Binning and Binning are of the view that the steps of Morrison plan were made for units in science. But with some improvement or modification these can be used in teaching at Social Studies. They wrote, while appreciating Morrison plan, "On evaluation of the process of Meristem, it comes to the knowledge easily that he made use of modern principles of education and the elements of teaching."

DISCUSSION UNIT METHOD

Discussion unit method is one of the various teaching methods of Social Studies. It is such a method which engages pupils mentally and physically in activities relating to education and enables them to adjust with new situations.

It is a system which makes teaching and learning effective. It is a means of instruction which brings about important modifications in pupils, by offering knowledge and experience. The extensive material of Social Studies is divided into main divisions and each such division is called a unit. Each related until should be so small as to enable pupils to easily understand it. A Unit can bring important modifications in pupils, in the form of knowledge and experiences which are integrated.

CHARACTERISTICS OF DISCUSSION UNIT METHOD

The following are the features of the discussion unit method:

1. The unit should be experimental.
2. The unit should be related with the entire syllabus.
3. Unit must be divided into smaller units so that the lesson becomes easier and clear.
4. Unit should be coordinated with social emotional and educational activities.
5. While framing the unit, attention should be paid to the level, class and time, at our disposal.
6. Unit must be based on pupil's previous knowledge.
7. Unit should neither be too small nor should it be too big.
8. Unit should be in the nature of guidance to the pupils.
9. Unit must be in accordance with the interest, needs and mental level of pupils.

MERITS OF DISCUSSION UNIT METHOD

1. It pays attention to the individual interest and problems of the child. Hence it does not insist on similar progress of success of all pupils. In it pupils get education in accordance with their individual differences.
2. This method has, not only the teachers' lecture and the text-book, but other supplementary material is also appropriately used.
3. In this method there is no specialisation of knowledge attempted, but the syllabus is fully generalised and presented before the pupils.
4. There is flexibility in it and as such full attention can be given to individual differences. The unit imparts knowledge of the entire lesson.
5. It trains in systematised deliberation and establishes relationships.

6. It develops logical thinking.
7. It develops in pupils proper aptitudes and interests and it develops social relationship amongst pupils.

DEMERITS OF DISCUSSION UNIT METHOD

1. It intraps pupils 'in futile discussion, owing to which time and efforts become wasteful. Noise and disorder continues to prevail in the class.
2. It is difficult to finish the entire syllabus in time, due to which often knowledge remains unclear and incomplete.
3. The success of this method depends upon efficient and trained teachers of which, unfortunately there is a great dearth.
4. Shy pupils, hesitate taking part in the discussion and owing to which talkative pupils overshadow the discussion.

MEANING OF PROBLEM SOLVING METHOD

It is not entirely a new method. Its use was made by ancient thinkers—like Socrates. But modem times, teachers and thinkers have accepted it as educational means. In it, mental conclusions are given more importance and there is deliberation and criticism. So, George Johnson writes, "The best course to train the mind is to present before the students real problems and for the solution of which opportunities and freedom are to be made available."

In modern times, some people accept the Problem solving method as a technique and others as a teaching method. Clark and Stone write, "None of us should call Problem Solving as a technique." This method tries to frode out solution scientifically of specific problem or difficulty. To explain its meaning, some definitions are given below.

Carter V. Good, "Problem method is a method of instruction by which learning is stimulated by the creation of challenging situations that demand solution."

John Dewey, "The real problem is contained in the fact which, though seemingly appear trifle and ordinary, yet makes the mind restless and challenging, rendering belief uncertain."

James M. Lee, "Problem solving is an educational device whereby the teacher-pupils attempt at a conscious, planned, purposeful efforts to arrive at an explanation or solution to some educationally significant difficulty. Problem solving is general educational method rather than a specific pedagogical technique."

ELEMENTS OF PROBLEM METHOD

1. Problems should be practical and useful.
2. It should have educational utility.
3. Its nature should be clear and definite.
4. It should be in accordance with the needs and (physical and mental) aptitudes of the pupils.
5. It should be related to social and physical environment.

STEPS IN PROBLEM METHOD

1. Selection of the Problem. The teacher and the pupils should together select the problem to be studied. It is necessary to get pupils' cooperation, all the more, because good results will not be achieved, unless they own up the problem. While selecting the problem, the teacher and the pupils should keep the following points in mind:

- The problem should be real.
- The problem should be important from the educational point of view.
- In other words let the problem offer to pupils opportunities to learn.
- The problem should be suitable for situation. Necessary instructions must be available therein.
- The problem should be related to the unit of the syllabus.

2. Why is it a Problem? After the selection of the problem, let the teacher induce the pupils to know why at all it is a problem? If there is only one answer to a question, then it cannot be a problem. For a problem, alternatives are a must. So, let the pupils see what different alternatives are present in the problem.

3. Finding out the Solution of the Problem. Pupils after collecting the required material, will find out some solution of the problem. This will be based upon established tested facts and principles. At the same time it will be clear and certain.

4. Carrying out the Problem. The entire class will work for the solution of the problem under the direction of the teacher. How to solve the problem? The decision will depend upon the nature of the problem *e.g.* if the nature of the problem is inductive, then inductive steps will be followed. If its nature is deductive, the steps concerning the same will be followed. So, according to the nature of the problem, pupils will collect relevant information. Subsequently, they will organise and analyse the same. The teachers' guidance will not be there to tell the solution, but will be related to its search and study needs besides difficulties to be tackled individually and collectively by the pupils.

5. Application of the Solution. The pupils should apply this solution in life, in the form of the class and individually. If they do not do so, they will be unable to adopt it in their own life and the work done by them in the school will be futile.

APPLICATION OF PROBLEM METHOD IN SOCIAL STUDIES

The problem method has an important place in the teaching of Social Studies, because its main object is to acquaint the pupils with the real problems of life. In this method either the teacher himself presents the problem before the pupils or the pupils themselves do it. The problem may be presented given by one pupil or many can do it collectively. But the stress is laid on the fact that the pupils understand it as their own and are eager to solve it. So, the selection of the problem should be made out of the social life of pupils. At the same time it should be according to their interest and mental level. Only then they will experience a sense of belongingness. The process of the problem will depend upon the nature of the problem. If it is deductive, then its steps will be different from the inductive one.

MERITS OF PROBLEM METHOD

1. Pupils learn to tackle social problems of their future life.
2. They learn to collect facts and organise them properly.
3. It helps in awakening respect for mutual views and the feeling of toleration.
4. It encourages them for self study and develops interest for extra and complementary study.
5. Scientific outlook develops in pupils.
6. They do not depend on blind imitation and on the habit of rote memory.
7. Pupils receive proper training for using the material in books and periodicals and find out truth and falsehood.
8. It develops self-reliance, confidence, self-study habits in pupils.
9. It saves pupils from becoming prey to prejudices/bias.
10. The pupils always remain active.
11. It develops pupils' mental faculty-reason, concept and contemplation and imagination.

DEMERITS OF PROBLEM METHOD

1. It is not useful for pupils at primary level, and can only be used in high classes.
2. It takes too much time. As a result, the syllabus cannot be finished in time.
3. It is not necessary that this method will yield satisfactory results.
4. It involves much expenditure.
5. Difficult problem creates disappointment in pupils.
6. It cannot be used for every topic.

7. It needs experienced and capable teachers, since average teacher cannot use it.
8. It is not possible to study the subject continuously and in a serial order.

LECTURE METHOD

This method has been used in education from ancient days. At pressant also this method has occupied an important place in Indian schools. The teacher, in it, teaches through telling. It is called Telling Method. For success, the lecture method depends upon two factors:

(a) The selection of the subject-matter, and

(b) The manner of presenting the subject-matter. The mode of presentation depends upon the personality of the teacher. For this, it is necessary for him to have proper preparation and suitable voice. Some progressive thinkers in education, are of the opinion that this method of teaching is unsuitable. But this argument does not appear to be correct, since this method is not opposed to the principles of psychology. There takes place some mental activity in the pupils. With full preparation the teacher can present the subject-matter in an interesting way and can ask question to keep them active. It all depends upon the teacher how he makes use of the method. Lecture accounts for alertness of auditory faculty. The lecture, along with personality of the speaker, finds place in the minds' of the pupils. For teaching Social Studies, this method is highly beneficial to the teacher makes use of story telling may to make the lecture interesting. Through his lecture, the teacher present before pupils, brief outlines of the topic in hand.

WHEN TO USE LECTURE METHOD

The teacher can use lecture/narration method, telling method for the following purposes:

1. ***To Motivate.*** Before presenting a lesson or a unit of the subject, the pupils can be encouraged to study the same, by explaining first, the important points through lecture

method. With this, their learning will be facilitated when the subject-matter will be presented.

2. ***To Summarize.*** Some pupils are up-set on seeing the extensiveness of the subject-matter. They find themselves unsuccessful to come out of the cobweb of the subject-matter. In such a case, they do not agree to study the extensive subject-matter. Hence it is necessary that this extensive subject-matter be presented in such a way so that the whole subject-matter be presented in a small form. This task can easily be done by lecture method. In addition, by presenting the subject matter in a brief form, the pupils can be given a broad knowledge of the subject-matter. Owing to this its study becomes meaningful when they read books. So, the use of the lecture method should be made to summarise the subject-matter.
3. ***To Save Time.*** It takes time to read and understand the text-book. In the same way modern methods of teaching also require time. With lecture method pupils' time can be saved. Through lecture, adequate subject-matter can be presented in short time. Hence, lecture method can be used also for saving the time of the pupils.
4. ***To Clarify.*** Lecture method can be used to explain the events, terms concepts and principles involved in the subject. It is only possible by lecture method to interpret. It is necessary to clarify them in simple words. So, lecture method can be adopted affectively.
5. ***To Present Additional Material.*** At times, the subject matter may be too briefing the books and may be insufficient. Looking at the level of the pupils, the teacher can give additional matter. So with the help of lecture method, the teacher can present additional material to pupils to add to their knowledge.
6. ***To Give Assignment.*** It is highly unpsychological to give home-work saying, "Write an essay on whatever you have learnt in the class. " In fact, for the usefulness of homework,

a brief lecture may be delivered on it relation to present subject-matter and how it may be done etc. While giving home-work, the teacher should make use of a lecture.

ADVANTAGES OF LECTURE METHOD

1. Individualised Instruction. It is based on lecture/narration method. The printed words in the book cannot tell much to the students. Books cannot pay attention to individual differences. But in lecture method, the teacher and the pupils sit face to face and carry out exchange of knowledge ideas. The subject-matter can adequately be made clear, as best as possible, through discussion; conversation, criticism in the course of give and take. The teacher can remove individual difficulties.

2. Classification of Subject-Matter. In this method, the subject-matter is made clear to the maximum. Many points come up in the subject-matter which are tough and complicated. The subject remains unqualified, on one reading. Through lecture method, the unqualified points can be reapeated again and again and can be expressed in other words, till it becomes clear to pupils.

3. Development of Logical Reasoning. This method develops reasoning and expression of students. Pupils reason with the speaker and analyse and comment on the principles theories presented by him and through discussion, resolve their doubts. Thus their reasoning power develops and they learn to express their ideas.

4. It Saves Time. If teaching is done by this method, it will save a lot of time and labour. Through lecturing, extensive subject-matter can be presented briefly in a short time. In the text-book method the pupils have to spend time and labour in reading the important and unimportant parts of the subject-matter. Through the lecture only the relevant subject-matter is presented in easy language, and their time and labour is saved.

5. Unit Method in Teaching of Social Studies/Science. To prepare introduction of a new topic, subject or unit this method is the best. With this method, topics like nationalisation of banks, inflation, satyagrah can be explained in a short time. The points/issues become clearer through lecture method. In addition, pupils' time can also be saved.

6. To make Subject-Matter Interesting and Effective. By this method, the teacher can make the subject interesting. In it the teacher can clarify the matter through interpretation and gestures. As compare with printed words, spoken words are more effective. At times the teacher can more effectively tell what he wants to tell to the class by his tone, gestures and facial expression.

7. Improvement in Pronunciation. It improves the pronunciation of the pupils. The pupils imitate the pronunciation of the teacher and improve their own expression.

8. Psychological in Nature. The teacher plans his lecture on psychological basis whereas the text-books are written on logical basis. Thus, the lectures are superior to text-books and according to child psychology.

9. Pupils and Teacher Remain Active. To some extent, both remain active. The teacher narrates and puts questions to pupils on the present problems.

10. Clarification of Home-Work. At the end of the lesson, pupils are given home-work. Mostly pupils do not attempt it. The main reason is that they do not understand what is to be done in respect of the home-work. The teacher briefly explains the home to through lecture.

DISADVANTAGES OF LECTURE METHOD

1. Pupils are Passive Listeners. It is not a natural method. Often the immature teacher, while lecturing, makes the pupils passive in the class. Such a teacher goes on lecturing and the pupils listen to him like statues. They do not take any interest in class teaching.

2. One Sided. From educational point of view this method is one sided. The pupil is not required to work as much as the teacher has to. In India the teacher has to deliver nearly six lectures per day. It is difficult for the teacher to prepare six lectures per day.

3. Stress on Theoretical Knowledge. It puts more emphasis on the theoretical knowledge of the subject. No importance is given to the practical part of knowledge. It does not assign any place to activity. It fully disregards, 'learning by doing' .

4. Lack of Real Knowledge. It is one thing to conduct real study and quite another to finish the syllabus. The lecture method can finish the syllabus quickly, but does not generate real learning.

5. Lack of Deep Study. Pupils do not get opportunity to carry out original study. They begin feeling contented with whatever subject-matter the teacher presents. Pupils do not learn to develop habits of self-study.

6. Unstable Knowledge. Knowledge gained by this method, does not become permanent since knowledge of this type has no relation with activity and is not related to practical work.

7. Limited Time. The attention span of the pupils is not so much, as to attentively listen to the lecture extending from 40 to 50 minutes.

8. Efficient Lecturer. The success of this method depends upon lecturing efficiency of the teacher. If this is not efficient, then he can never teach effectively.

9. Useful for High Classes. It does not work successfully in lower classes. It can be used more profitably in higher classes.

10. Teaching becomes Dull. It makes teaching activity dull and uninteresting. The teaching-learning process becomes one way.

PRECAUTIONS IN USING THE LECTURE METHOD

While employing this method, the teacher should bear the following points in mind.

1. Proper Planning. Before delivering a lecture, the subject-matter should be properly planned. The lecture can never be successful unless the subject-matter is planned. He should have the ability to satisfactorily answer all types of questions, raised in the class.

2. Synopsis of the Lecture. Before lecturing he should prepare its synopsis or outline. This will facilitate in learning the main points.

3. Capable Teacher. As far as possible, teachers should develop lecturing ability. He should be a good speaker. He should be such as to modify his pronunciation, facial expressions etc. according to the topic.

4. Other Suggestions:

(a) Should try to lecture in the form of a free talk.

(b) Background and introduction should be prepared.

(c) While lecturing, he should note the facial expression of pupils, it will tell him, if the pupils are understanding or not.

(d) Should speak steadily and in a composed way. In between let there be pauses.

(e) He should pay particular attention to his pronunciation, language, style. defacial expression.

(f) In between teacher should ask questions and it will keep pupils attentive, and hert in the course of the lecture.

(g) There should be no tension. It should not be dry.

(h) At relevant places, teacher should take the help of examples, anecdotes etc.

(i) Due place should be assigned for evaluation under lecture method.

MODERN METHODS

Educators have fixed the development of all the facilities of students as their main aim. To achieve this aim, the educationists have developed various methods of teaching. The bases of these methods is to put on pupils the responsibility of self-learning. Every pupil has some or other aptitudes. The chief aim of modern education is to explore such aptitudes for, development. To receive instruction, pupils should have interest in it. They will acquire the knowledge of subject-matter if they have interest. Modern psychologists have pointed out that pupils receive best education:

1. Through observation and inspection.
2. By establishing relationship.

3. Through problem solving.
4. By experimenting.
5. Through creative activity.
6. By exchange of views.

All these are useful in receiving instruction in Social Studies. These methods are known as Activity Methods or Modern Methods.

DISCUSSION METHOD

According to modern educational thought the child is not considered mere passive listener, but emphasis is put on his active participation in teaching-learning process. Teaching methods are employed from the point of view of keeping the child active. Of these, Discussion Method is one. It is the one, in which the teacher and the pupils carry out, exchange of views relating to some topic, question or problem. Thus, knowledge method gained through exhaustive logical discussion, is known as Discussion Method. In discussion, generally, important ideas or problems are included. Discussion is not a stock of necessary and meaningless facts, but is logical knowledge as result of exchange of thoughts. While criticising it some people say that discussion is another form of lecturing. Some others find fault with this method, that it is meant for imposing one view point on others. But in fact it is not that. It is entirely different from others. To explain its meaning more fully, some definitions are as under:

James M. Lee, "Discussion is an educational group activity in which the teacher and pupils (Students) cooperatively talk over some problem or topic."

Sattlere & Miller, "Discussion is a reflective thinking by two or more persons who cooperatively exchange information and ideas in efforts to solve a problem or to gain better understanding of a problem."

Yaokam & Simpson, "Discussion is a special form of conversation. It is an exchange of ideas of a more reasoned, detailed kind, than that found in ordinary conversation and generally involves the conversation of important ideas and issues."

ESSENTIAL PARTS OR CONSTITUENTS OF DISCUSSION

The following is the description of its essential parts:

1. The Leader. There is no doubt that the teacher himself is the director and the leader. He should, as a leader, do adequate preparation before starting discussion. For example, what should be selected for discussion and how to Plan it, he has to decide in advance. Generally it is experienced that many teachers go on speaking themselves and endeavour to dominate the whole scene. He should encourage all pupils to take part in the discussion and should guide the pupils if they find difficulty in expressing their thoughts.

2. The Content. The teacher and the pupils should cooperatively decide the problem or the subject for discussion. It should be in accordance with the understanding and within the access of the pupils, so that they may easily participate in it. The use of books, periodicals, newspaper, picture, maps and many other kinds of things should be made in the course of the discussion. The teacher should take the responsibility to procure the required material.

3. The Group. Ordinarily, in the group there are pupils having different ideas. It is the duty of the teacher to encourage every pupil to participate in the discussion. It is also seen that in the beginning shy children and those with low intelligence, get nervous. If at the promptings of the teacher, they try to speak, brilliant pupils make fun. The teacher should see that such an occasion does not arise. He should carefully list the views of children with low intelligence and should appreciate them.

PROJECT METHOD

No method has evoked mare interest than the Project Method. The term project in education came in use during, the early years .of this century and is a modern contribution to educational theory and practice. It is the outcome of philosophy of education and is a natural extension of the problem method. But the credit of unit acting this method goes to Professor William Kilpatrick, who has defined it as "a whole-hearted purposeful activity, proceeding in a social environment." Dr. J.A. Stevenson who perfected it as a method of teaching.

According to him, "A project is a problematic act carried to completing in its natural setting." It is, in fact, that, form of coordinated activity which is directed towards the learning of a significant skill or process. It also involves the acquisition of useful information and also affects attitudes and interests.

Dr. W.H. Kilpatrick of Columbia University defined Project as "Whole hearted purposeful activity proceeding in a social environment". J.A. Stevenson gave a definition that relates to the teaching of Agriculture of the early years. He states that a project is it problematic at carried to completion in its natural setting. He has not been able to explain as to what constitutes a natural setting in the educational process. Billard defines, "A project is a bit of rear life that has been imparted into the school."

From the point of view of Social Studies, the term should be restricted to a pupil-planned, purposeful task, accomplished in a real life like situation. It is a reaction against dull, mountainous, purposeless and lifeless class-room teaching.

BASIC PRINCIPLES OF THE PROJECT METHOD

Project method is based on the following principles:

1. The Principle of Purpose. Effective learning is possible only when the child is interested in purpose full earning and for this:

(a) The school work should be related to child's out-side life and

(b) The child should realise that he can achieve some purpose or objective in pursuing that work.. Only then they will put their life and soul in the educational task. They take little interest in an activity which is aimless or which is not purposeful or which does not combine life with learning. The success of any project is largely determined by the degree to which the pupils identify themselves with it and adopt it as their own.

2. The Principle of Activity. Mere securing interest of the child is not sufficient. Because every child is active by nature and physical and mental experiences derived from activity are more educative and retentive. A child should be given ample opportunities—for working on things, projects and these should be profitably exploited for education.

3. The Principle of Reality. Children should be provided with those activities which look like real life situations. If education is a preparation for life, the school must create real life situations in the school premises. They should be made to learn to solve actually life situations and problems. Because life itself is full of projects and problems.

4. The Principle of Experience. Physical and mental activities provide experience and should be such as are useful to the children for educational purposes. When a child works in groups he learns to cooperate with others and thus share their interests and purposes. He gets valuable social experiences in cooperative living, character building and practical democracy and citizenship.

5. The Principle of Utility. The knowledge gained through any educational activity must be useful and practical. Doing various activities alone is not important. Their importance lies in their practical utility. Project ensures this because activity is done in actual life-situations and achieves best educational results.

6. The Principle of Freedom. The desire to learn should grow out of pupil's own needs and purposes. The desire for any activity should be spontaneous and not forced by the teacher. The project should grow out of the child's own interests and purposes and a child should be free to plan and do things. There should be no fixed time-table and no rigid curriculum. The children should be left to themselves in an atmosphere of freedom—freedom to choose the activity according to their capacities and mental power. There should be no impositions and restrictions.

Procedure of a Project

There are different steps in the project though these may not be clearly visible in all cases but they are there in all projects. Every project has six steps.

1. Providing a Situation for the Selection of the Project. The teacher of Social Studies should first know the interest and aptitude of the students and then he is to provide them a situation involving a problem affecting society. He is to leave the students to examine, observe and study the problem from all aspects and realize the necessity and importance of solving it. The teacher's job is to provide such a situation according to the pupil's interest and aptitude as may give them spontaneous urge to carry out a project. Situations caliber created by conversation, discussion, pictures, stories, visits and excursion, etc. Students may then be prompted to choose the project after having examined several situations. When the children make unsuitable choice, the teacher should direct and guide, them and explain to them the difficulties and undesirability of the project selected by them and to persuade them to take up some other suitable project.

2. Purposing. This is a very important step in a project. "The most important thing about it is that the pupils do the purposing". There is a tendency on the part of some teachers to choose the project for their students and making them to accept the choice but such an effort has very little educative value. If the project has been proposed by them they will be able to plan and carry out in a better way.

3. Judging the Project. This is a stage, where the students review their work and try to find out what mistakes they have made in planning or in carrying out the project. It is a sort of self-criticism which is a very important form of training and should never be neglected.

4. Planning and Executing the Project. Under the able and expert guidance of the teacher the students will plan out the project. The teacher has to the students the necessity of planning. For this purpose oral discussions should be held among the students for execution, the teacher should assign the work to students according to their ability and interest.

5. Self-criticism-evaluation. Self-criticism includes the choice of the project, its planning, duties assigned to right type of students, difficulties felt. How to avoid these mistakes in future and how to improve them in future? They learn to criticise their own work. Whether or not the aim was achieved? Whether the goal set was achieved? The evaluation of the project should be made, in the first instance, by the pupils and afterwards by the teacher.

6. Recording of the Work Done. The children record their findings in their note-books. They should put down a complete record of all the activities connected with the project.

Merits of the Project Method

1. *Based on the Laws of Learning.* The most outstanding merit of the Project Method is that it is based on the ways of learning which take into consideration the best conditions under which the child can learn and remember for a long time what a child learns. These laws are:

(a) Law of readiness states that mind of the child should be made ready for learning and for acquiring knowledge. In his context, wise selection of a project prepares the child's mind for the work he is about to do.

(b) The law of effect requires that learning should be accompanied by happiness and satisfaction. By doing practical work the child gets pleasure and satisfaction.

(c) Law of exercise requires the child to practise what he has learnt. The project method in fact is based on learning by doing. Actual doing of things gives effective knowledge.

2. *Education is Related to Life and Surroundings.* Under the Project Method, we relate the school life to social life and education is given according to the conditions prevailing in life. Only those projects in Social Studies are selected which suit to the child's everyday relies and experiences. Social sciences have been made interesting and learning of these subjects is no more boring because knowledge gained is real, practical and useful, leading to the formation of proper habits and attitudes. A great deal of incidental learning takes place as the project is pursued.

3. It Inculcates Self-Reliance. The Project Method teaches self-reliance and responsibility to the students. They learn to be self-dependent when they are required to make their own decisions affecting their economic and social life.

4. *Dignity of Labour.* The Project Method upholds the dignity of labour and imbibes in the students a feeling of respect for all the workers. In real life situations, the students will be required to do all types of work with their own hand, including manual work and thus it upholds the dignity of labour.

5. *It Imparts Training for Democratic Way of Life.* It encourages the students to cooperate, to think and to act together for a common purpose. In this way, they acquire foresight, power of judgement, independence of thought and action initiative, responsibility, tolerance, self-respect, etc. It, thus, inculcates right type of social habits and prepares the future citizen to live in a democratic community. All these are useful social habits which impart real training in citizenship and a democratic way of life.

6. *This Method is Economical.* This method is economical in the sense because they learn more and much be term in the short-time. Economy in learning is there because there is no strain and worry and they feel less tired as the project is of their own choice. It yields the best results in the shortest possible time and with the least wastage of energy.

7. *No Cramming and Memory Work.* It discards and discourages cram work because various projects are assigned in the form of problems. Knowledge becomes effective because it is not imparted as a finished thought product of the teacher. It is gained as it by-product of socially useful activities. Students learn social ideas by doing things themselves. This inculcates problem solving attitudes and develop thinking and reasoning power of the child.

8. *Correlation of Subjects and Unity or Curriculum.* All social sciences have been correlated. We do not find any artificial and water-tight division of the various social sciences which form the unity of curriculum. Knowledge of various social sciences is gained in correlated manner.

Limitations and Demerits of this Method

1. *Educative aspect of Social Studies is Neglected.* Most of the teachers of Social sciences opine that this method implies the making of models or doing hand work. It is argued that in this method the educative aspect of the project is neglected to some extent. Knowledge is gained in a haphazard and scrappy manner it disturbs the logical arrangement of subject-matter of social sciences. This method tries to bind many loose ends of social sciences and thus many concept terms cannot be bound or linked together by using this method.

2. *Shirkers are Mere Onlookers.* There are certain students who are tempted to shoulder all the responsibility and other students may remain in the background. There are shirkers and may tend to be merely onlookers and also remain in the background. For all this, the teacher should see that every student does something or the other and all the students work in co-operation with one another.

3. *Knowledge Acquired is not Systematic.* Knowledge acquired through this method is not systematic, logical and orderly to proper development of various concepts of social-sciences and it is not possible to establish sequence of various social events. Even the most carefully selected projects cannot cover the entire syllabus of social studies.

4. *This is a Costly Method.* This method is costly one and requires a lot of material which is neither available easily nor an ordinary school has the requisite funds available for its implementation. This method is, thus, simply unsuitable for most of the schools in India. Most of the projects become activities only.

5. *Difficulty of Suitable Text-books of Social Studies.* Another difficulty is that of the difficulty of suitable text-books in Social Studies are available which contain groups of projects and wherein selection of projects is made possible with certainty.

STORY TELLING METHOD

One of the most important methods of teaching social studies—particularly the history part of this subject is story telling. The children in the primary classes should be told stories of great men and women and of early man, stories of famous rulers, reformers, writers, saints, discoverers and scientists, stories of scripts, numbers, trade, money. Story telling is an art which aims at presenting to the pupils through the medium of story clear, vivid interesting, ordered sequence of events. Their minds should be able to reconstruct these happenings. Varied types of stories as myths, legends, moral fables and true historical tales can be used for lending colour to personalities and events. The type of stories and the manner of their narration will vary with the age of children. They should be able to live in imagination through the experiences recounted, either as spectators or possibly as participators. As an actor and speaker, the teacher can make the lessons lively and interesting to the pupils who can visualise the events and personalities described.

Use of Story Telling in Different Stages

The method of teaching history, a part of social studies should be mainly the story method upto class V. Stories and anecdotes otherwise enliven the subject-matter as the child advances in age and understanding, in the middle and secondary classes using other methods as Lecture or Conversation method or even discussion and problem method while telling of related stories will make the subject-matter interesting and lively.

Hints for effective use of this method. Story should be told in orderly manner.

1. *Ordely Manner.* Expressions like "Oh, I forget to tell you about an important point" does not speak of a good story teller. The teacher must know the story fully well.

2. *Full of Action and Details.* The story should be replete with descriptions of places, persons and things with frequent reference to geographical conditions during the narration of stories.

3. *Interesting Narration.* Story telling can be made interesting by the use of catchy words and phrases and handy illustrations such as metaphors and similes and correlation with the verbal experiences with which children are familiar. Catchy' words and phrases create proper images. Narration can be made interesting if the narrator takes the role of one of the characters.

4. ***Suitability.*** Narration should be suitable to the audience. Although the facts should never be distorted the narration should be adapted to the audience.

Advantages of Story Telling

1. ***Enhancing Interest in the Subject.*** Story telling is the most effective way of bringing out all the aspects—cultural and social, economic of prehistoric, ancient and medieval societies.
2. ***Inculcation of Virtues.*** Story telling is the best ally for helping in developing virtues in pupils including the much coveted traits of character as piety, truthfulness, valour, charity, etc. The teacher can very easily achieve success in this objective by relating the life-stories of great personalities to the pupils.
3. ***Requirements from the teacher.*** Story telling is an wet. Every social studies teacher should know this art. For this he should have rich imagination, accurate and wide knowledge of the past and a rich collection of stories to use them as and when the situation demands.
4. ***Development of Imagination.*** A good story fires the imagination of listeners. It takes them away from the matter-of-fact world. It offers ample scope for the play of their imagination.

TEXT-BOOK METHOD

Defined as "that teaching procedure in which the mastery of the text-book is the immediate objective." Text-book method means the procedure which "revolves around the text-book just as another procedure might revolve around the problem or the project". However, we may find good as well as bad teaching within the limits of the text-book method.

While text-book is a very useful means of getting incise and up-to-date information, an oral lesson may become lengthy, complicated and unintelligible. A text-book is logically and systematically arranges the subject-matter for students.

Use of text-book in social studies. If the teacher bases all of his leaching upon a single text-book, the text-book procedure may become undesirable. As generally followed in schools in this procedure the teacher or one of the students, reads the text-book in the class. The teacher explains difficult words and sentences and removes flaws in reading and pronunciation. While suitable in language teaching this procedure is highly objectionable in case of Social Studies. Text-book is not an end in itself but only a means. A text-book is an effective aid and must be taken as such. One text-book should never be completely depended upon. To supplement the subject-matter given in one particular text-book other text-books, references and resources should also be consulted.

Advantages of Text-Book in Social Studies

1. ***Meeting the Need of the Students.*** From the students point of view, a text-book should meet their requirements by the use of simple language, headings, sub-headings, questions, assignments, maps, charts, pictures and other illustrative material.

2. ***Developing Study Skills.*** Provides a common basis on which the process of reading, analysing outlining and summarising can be mastered. A text-book furnishes a common laboratory in which study skills can be developed. By studying the text-book independently at home and understanding its content the student develops study skills.

3. ***Suggesting Application of the Material.*** A text-book suggests application of the subject-matter, through assignments, drills, questions, projects and other activities in social studies.

4. ***Reflecting and Establishing Standards.*** A text-book indicates what the teacher is required to teach and what the pupils are supposed to learn in social studies. By its teaching and learning aids, text-book greatly affects methods and establishes the standards of scholarship. It furnishes a definite basis for specific assignments, problems, and projects. Through it the teacher can easily establish class as well as individual standards.

5. *Giving an Accurate Account of the Subject.* A text-book is very useful as it gives a reasonably correct logical and systematic account of the subject field in an organised manner.

6. *Expanding and Limiting its Scope and Size, According to Needs.* According to the changing needs of education a textbook can expand and delimit its scope, size and content. Sometimes it leads and sometimes follows the educational process.

7. *Presenting Different and Opposing Points of View on Historical and Current Events.* A text-book presents history and current affairs in such a way as to develop in pupils an appreciation of different points of view.

8. *Basis of Almost all Other Methods.* As all post all other methods can be used with the text-books as a basis of study assignment procedure or telling and discussion method or even problem, project and unit methods can be used with advantage with the help of a text-book.

9. *Presenting Content, Relating to Human Relationship.* Giving an accurate account of our environment, the values and principles which guide our actions and the processes through which we hope to improve ourselves. A social studies text-book helps in improving the physical and mental well-being of our pupils.

Limitations of the Text-Book

1. *Rote Memorisation.* Students generally memories text-book word for word and reproduce the same in black and white at the time of examination. Accepting blindly what is given in the text -book they feel that it contains all the needed information and knowledge. However, enriched scholarship of the teacher can be a suitably guarantees against this limitation.

2. *Contains Only Minimum Essential.* Containing only a summary treatment of the subject-matter a text-book does not give lively details. It, thus, leaves a lot to be done by the teacher. Without teacher's planning and direction the students cannot derive full advantage of the text-book.

3. *Possibility of Errors of Detail and Interpretation.* There is a possibility of errors of detail and interpretation as the whole field of subject-matter in a text-book is to be condensed and encompassed by an author to meet the requirements of students. This defect can be removed if the teacher is competent enough to correct errors and counteract prejudiced interpretations.

4. *Tendency to Dominate.* Because of its definite and convenient subject-matter a text-book may dominate the entire procedure of teaching. Covering a certain number of pages the students and teachers may drift into the habit of routine procedure accepting anything that they see in print. This limitation can also be overcome by the utilization of other aids.

Thus, too much reliance should not be placed upon the text-book. The text-book method is not a complete method in itself. The teacher should make to liberalise the lecture method and the supplementary references, maps, charts, pictures and other aids and materials to supplement text-book. In classes where a single text-book is used the pupils should be encouraged to make use of a variety of supplementary materials, according to their interests and abilities. Challenging assignments should be given to meet their individual differences and to facilitate their learning, so as to motivate the pupil for self-activity in learning.

SOCIALIZED RECITATION METHOD OF TEACHING SOCIAL STUDIES

There have been very important changes in the field of educational methodology. Parents, educators, educational administrators, all have felt the hopelessness of the age-old practices of teaching in our schools. They have found the old passive methods as educationally unsound, creating many problems for the teachers and the education traditionally, has been in way of process, meaning flow of knowledge and information from the teacher to students. This made the learning prove monotonous and boring and created discipline problems too. This drilling facts by the teacher in the mind of pupils is resented to by the educationists and the educands.

Passivity to Activity

The modern advancements in education and psychology have a fundamental change in educational methodology. In place of this change in the classroom, emphasis have been laid on pupil activity. It is to make the learners, the certain educational process. Education is conceived as acquisition of knowledge or facts. We laid emphasise on developing attitudes through classroom teaching and proceedings. So with the socialisation of educational process we must cry for socialised curriculum and methods.

The effect of this socialisation has been very marked on teaching of Social Studies which has been taking main social view point in consideration. So to fulfil the aims of Social Studies we must attempt at adopting these socialised teachings so far as possible.

So socialized recitation is the atmosphere of teaching which enables the pupils to learn in socialized atmosphere which gives them the opportunity to develop or practise the skill, ability and attitudes necessary for social participation.

Objectives of Socialised Techniques

The objectives of socialised recitation are derived from social nature. It increases the ability of the pupils to learn by doing or by actual life experiences. This learning by doing and learning by living makes them undertake joint and group work. It teaches the pupils to work together in a friendly, cooperative manner developing their social consciousness. When the children work with things and with people they learn to shoulder responsibility and to discharge the responsibility in an evident manner. So in them is developed a sense of responsibility and duty.

Also we find that our traditional class room atmosphere is from and there are no clear and close understanding among the teachers and the students. Their lessons too are formal. So the personal effect of the teachers personality is not visible. Socialised recitation reduces this formality and helps in establishing friendly feelings between the teacher and the taught. Some people have negative self-feelings in them due to their social, mental and physical defects. Socialized teaching helps them in social participation and makes the naturally handicapped pupils to become more self-confident. Moreover, the children do recognise the merits of others and this makes them respectful to one another.

Capacity for Clear and Responsible Thinking

Socialized teaching has made pupil, to analyse and judge from the different view points the relative merits and demerits of various social problems. This develops in them the capacity for clear and responsible thinking, and of comprehensive planning for the future. They are better prepared for the hardships of adult life where they have to deal with the intricacies of politics or economics or cultural pursuits.

Class Organization

The socialized classroom is permeated by a friendly spirit of cooperative work. There should be a proper nodal setting in the class room and members should have the feelings of mutual confidence and respect among themselves, The seating arrangement of the class is not of the traditional type but the seats are arranged in small groups or in a semi-circular form as may be needed for group discussion or group work. Long rows of seats with teacher's desk prominently placed of the type of a lecture room are hardly to be found The seats should be arranged including the teacher's desk also among the pupils desks.

In a socialized classroom the pupils participation is not a premium. As Yoakam and Simpson have remarked, "Children are discussing, questioning, reporting, planning and working in natural ways. It does not matter much what the seating arrangement is or where the teachers. What matters is the spirit with which the students, and the teacher work. The teacher is no overlord of the class, the controlling factor in it, but on the other hand, he is one of the members of the class or group. He is first among the members exercising his leadership but keeps his authority in abeyance. He is no more the chief actor in the classroom drama.

Plan of Socialized Procedure

The socialized recitation may be described as "Social Discussion", but the main problem arises, what should be the forms of these plans of discussions. These may be divided into four broad categories:

1. Informal Group Plan
2. The Formal or Institutionalised Group Plan
3. Self-directing Group Plan
4. Seminar Group Plan

1. ***Informal Group Plan.*** In the informal group plan, the discussion on the social problem is Informal. There is free exchange of knowledge and experience for common interests. The teacher and the pupils discuss about the problems and projects rather informally. There is no regular procedure. Sometimes, the teacher leads the discussion and than other time some students may perform the duties of the leader of discussion. There is a free exchange of information, thought or opinion on a particular topic.

    Everyone is free to ask explanation, volunteer information and to report or to investigate into the interest of the group to which one belongs. This plan is very useful for beginners and youngsters who do not understand the intricate organizational patterns.

2. ***Institutionalised Group Plan.*** In institutional group plan, the children imitate the adult forms of institutions like clubs, councils, senate, etc. All formalities such as election of the president and office-bearers take place. They elect the class officers, maintain the records and form committees. It requires several leaders everyday. The lesson is divided into a number of parts and is chosen for each part with a number of assisting members. Sometimes they so arrange that the committees prepare their work under the supervision of their leaders. They prepare an outline of their work and put before the class. The topic leader is the

leader of the house for the time and discussions are arranged. Different members explaining their own view points, giving and receiving the needed information. The planning is approved by the teacher of Social Studies. This trains pupils how to participate in the organisational life and prepares them for the duties of citizenship. The teacher is to see that the students do not go astray and equal chances of leadership and expression are available to all. This institutionalized group plan may take two important fulfils, the Panel System and Symposium discussion plan.

(i) *Symposium.* It is a type of group discussion where two or more persons present to the audience separate papers or speeches concerning a problem or different phases of a problem. After the learned speakers have delivered speeches or read out their papers, the audience are free to ask questions, to seek information and explanation and to contribute additional information. The symposium presents a broader basis for discussion. The teacher or the pupil may perform the presidential functions. Her job will be to introduce the topic and the speakers.

(ii) *The Panel System.* We adopt panel system when we have a large number of members. We select a few learned and well informed members. They sit in front of the audience. They talk, discuss over the problem with one another and majority of people are mere on-lookers. The panel members through their speeches, papers, questions, cross questions, answers and discussion make the problem clear. At the end, the president summarises the discussion and throws open discussion to the house for suggestion. Thus, great chances of speech and discussion are available to the selected members.

3. ***Self-Directing Group Plan.*** In a self-directing group plan the technique is an informal consideration of problems or ideas and its main purpose is to get suggestion or consensus of members participating in the group. The group meets first and then it is split into smaller groups. Different aspects of a social or historical problem are assigned to these smaller groups. Co-operation, courtesy and control is self-imposed throughout the action. These smaller groups present the findings the act solution of the group problem one by one to the whole group. Some social scientist is invited to work as a resource person, who given his expert and mature opinion or advice on his will thought views on the problem.
4. ***The Seminar Group Plan.*** The seminar group plan is mostly needed the college and university stage. A group of students are noted a problem for investigation and they offer their findings for group discussion and criticism. The periodic report and discussion are held, their reports are critically evaluate in the group conference. Thus, students plan, organize, investigate, and report, are discuss and evaluate. This gives the training in self-learning, and promotes independent thought. This method can also be adopted at the high school stage. The teacher should generally take up the fole of the class leader being most informed and most read.

Teacher and His Role in Socialized Recitation

The success of the socialized technique depends totally on the teacher who is the pivot and the centre of all class activity. He can perform his duties well only when he is familiar with the social experience of pupils, their social and culture background and their attitudes. He should have the qualities of leadership and initiative. Not only that, he should be able to inspire others. He is to conduct the operative activities of the class and himself must have faith in this. He is to plan a series of activities where the need of cooperative activities does. He is to develop attitudes interests and ideals in the students.

Also, he is to provide them much needed information skills, habits, necessary for successful participation in socialized activity. He himself should be kind, sympathetic, respectful to children's personality but at the same time the strong and persistent.

Merits of this Method

1. This method imparts training to the students in learning social values and social manners. It develops right attitudes, which is a major aim of teaching social studies.
2. It makes them good nationals and good citizens. They learn to adjust the environment or with social milieu and with other members of their immunity. It trains students for participation in a social environment. It stimulates groups consciousness.
3. This method promotes physical, mental and social activities. It makes the children think, analyse and judge. He thus, helps in the development of their thinking and reasoning faculties.
4. Professors Yoakam and Simpson have enumerated the outcomes or advantages of the socialized recitation as follows:

   "1. Pupils learn to plan activities

   2. Common interests and purposes are discovered

   3. Practice in leadership is gained

   4. Initiative is encouraged

   5. Independence of thought is achieved

   6. Pupils learn to take part in discussion

   7. Practice is given in passing judgement

   8. Training in courtesy is given

   9. Ability to report is developed

   10. Extensive experience is made possible

11. Self-confidence is gained.
12. Teachers know pupils better
13. Pupils have greater admiration and respect for teachers
14. Learning is more highly motivated.
15. Respect for others is developed
16. Cooperation is learned

Limitations of this Method

This method is not free from shortcomings, but can be used a supplementary device.

1. ***It can in no Way, Replace all other Methods of Teaching.*** At last, it can be used as supplementary device and its use as a method of teaching in Social Studies, especially in civics is very great. Whatever, criticism can be levied is all against the extreme view and abuse.

2. ***Dominating Students may Monopolies Discussion.*** There is always a danger that certain dominating students may monopolies all discussion and leave little scope for other children to participate. Such domination is not conducive to the full values that should result from the use of this method. It is, thus, the duty of the teacher of Social Studies to plan recitation in such a way that the discussion is not monopolised by a few students.

3. ***Inadequate Mastery of Subject-matter.*** It is alleged that this method leads to inadequate mastery of subject-matter of Social sciences. There is little of logical arrangement and also certain important points not get proper emphasis and certain other unimportant minor details are over emphasised on which the students waste their time.

4. ***Danger in Exclusive use of Socialized Recitation.*** Exclusive use of this method for teaching of Social Studies is a dangerous move. Of course, in every lesson of Social Studies, the students should be given chances to participate in one or other form of social recitation. Combination with other methods and procedures can be used very successfully in the classroom.

DALTON PLAN 1928

Miss Parkhurst tested her plan in various schools and was convinced of its fundamental soundness, though experience caused certain modifications and adaptations to meet difficulties which arose in practice.

In 1920, the plan was first introduced in a High School of a town called Dalton in U.S.A. Visitors from all over the world came to see its working and were greatly impressed and welcomed it. Especially in English educational circles, the plan was appreciated and its principles were discussed at certain conferences and results of its adoption in different schools were obtained which formed a very valuable part of educational literature.

Dalton Plan as an Organisation

It may be remembered that the Dalton plan is not a new method of teaching but a new method of organisation to provide opportunities to students, to learn more effectively than they did under the old system. The class as a unit of organisation may remain, but it does not remain a unit of instructions. Dalton plan lays emphasis on individual learning. A student may be promoted to next class at any time in the academic year when he or she has satisfactorily completed the year's work. For example, a student may be in 7th class in English and in 6th class in Mathematics according to his/her achievement under the Dalton plan. This means that the quick students may do it in shorter period and weak students may take more time.

Freedom in Organization

It is very essential to note the importance of freedom in organisation. The student must be left free to work as he likes. There is no time-table and students read, write and finish their work as they like.

Assignments or Contracts

In the Dalton plan, the syllabus in each subject for the whole year is divided into suitable monthly amounts by the teacher concerned.

In this division of work, consideration of holidays, the need of revision at certain stages and other such points are kept in view so that monthly amount shall be completed within the month in which it is expected to be completed. These monthly units are called contracts or assignments and all must be completed within the time allotted. In the allotment of time the intelligence, interest and aptitude of the students is well kept in view and if a student is unable to complete it within the required time she is asked to continue with it. Next assignment is not allotted unless the first one is completed. A proper check is made to avoid 'rush ahead' student is most interested. It is sometimes suggested that the student must complete all the assignments in different subjects before he takes up next assignment in any other subject.

Slow and rapid students can move at their own speed because there are no fixed periods. Ringing of bells has no place in Dalton plan. A student continues his work in any particular subject of study as long as he feels interested in that subject. Also a student can devote more time to the subjects or subjects in which his achievement is deficient. Students study what they like and not, what the teacher wants them to study.

The Promise

Before beginning the first monthly assignment of the yearly contract, each child usually signs a promise to complete the work. But in some schools, it has now been found unnecessary to insist on it. This is done to bring sanctity and sincerity to the work of students and to bind them morally.

Freedom in Work

The Dalton plan is characterized by free student activity. The old concept of silence in classroom is absent. They are free to move about the room, to talk and discuss with their class-mates and also to consult their teacher individually for their problems. There is no necessity of periodical examinations because the teacher can judge them from their work. It also provides for natural motivation in learning. No external motivation is necessary.

The Teacher—A Guide

The teacher should plan out properly by giving necessary references. His duty is to watch and guide each child in his re-adjustment to the altered school environment and machinery. In Dalton plan, the teacher plays less important role as regards teaching. He is required to give advice when sought. He is not to interfere unless wanted by the pupil.

Subject Rooms and Subject Teachers

Instead of classrooms, the school consists of subject rooms. The subject teacher is incharge of subject room. The subject teacher is in his room for the whole work day and all books, charts, maps diagrams and other material relating to the subject are in the same room and not in the library. The pupils can enter and leave the room as and when they like. There are no fixed periods and no classroom. No time table and no limit to the time that a student spends in a particular room.

Record of Work

In order to know how a child is working in one particular subject and in his class, records are maintained. They are in the form of graphs which help the student to see what progress he has made. The teacher can also keep a check on the progress of each child's work and to advise whose work is falling behind the other students.

Characteristics of Dalton Plan

The characteristics of the plan may be summarised as:

1. Curriculum is divided into units of work or assignments.
2. Students enter into contract to complete these assignments in the prescribed period and are at liberty to study the different subjects, how and when they please.
3. The progress of work is recorded by graphs.
4. Subject rooms and subject teachers replace classrooms and class teachers.

Limitations of the Dalton Plan

Many teachers in the West, however, have found by experience that a less rigid adoption of the Dalton plan is preferable.

1. There is still a need and place for the classroom teaching in inspiration lessons in social studies.
2. The Dalton plan is unsuitable for an average child. All the students, if left to progress at their own rate, cannot progress because the capacity of independent work is very rarely found in average students. It discourages and disheartens the average student.
3. It provides no opportunity for the development of the mind by a rapid inter-change of questions and answers. Many good teachers speak of the valuable training afforded by discussion of a problem in a Socratic way, to enable them to examine their quantum of knowledge and to express themselves with care and precision.
4. This plan is unsuitable for shirkers in work. In cooperative work they merely copy down the results of others and thus make little progress.
5. The plan of the school building and the variety of subjects offered by an ordinary Indian High School are great obstruction to the adoption of this plan. In India, most of the high schools are overcrowded due to large number of students and small classrooms. Suitable building is a great problem for most of the schools.
6. Difficulty of suitable text-books and reference books is another factor hampering the progress and work in Dalton plan. There are very few good reference books for Indian schools. The number of schools and institutions is so great that we cannot provide adequate libraries in a small number of years.

❐

3

Curriculum and Contents

According to modern concept, curriculum is the sum total of experiences, activities or the realities of life. In this respect, there is the assemblage of situations in which the child participates and faces them. We can say that curriculum is much more than the text-books, subject-matter and courses of study. 'Curriculum' is the term which stands for all these derived from the Latin word curie which means to run. So, curriculum means the 'road on which a person runs to reach some goal.' From this angle, 'education' is a race which makes one to run on the path of curriculum and through this the aim of the development of the personality of the child is reached.

According to K.B. Rudiyard and H.K.Henry, "Curriculum in its broadest sense includes the complete school environment involving all the courses, activities; readings and associations furnished to the pupils in the school."

According to Crow and Crow, "Curriculum covers total experience, which he gets in and out the school and which are involved in such programmes that help in his mental, physical, emotional, social, spiritual and moral development."

On the basis of these definitions we can say that for achieving aims of education what is done in an organised way, in and outside the school, comes under curriculum.

NEED AND IMPORTANCE OF CURRICULUM

Every society and nation has its own values, assumptions and needs for the fulfilment of which education is imparted and the goals are fixed for the same. Knowledge of those subjects and training in activities which are deemed necessary for the fulfilment of these goals are given proper place in the curriculum. So, for planned education, curriculum is a must. We see the importance of the same as under:

1. Education Process becomes Systematic. Curriculum decides teaching material. With the help of this, it is made clear what knowledge of subjects and how much efficiency in activities be got and at what level of education. Thus, a precise curriculum makes educational activities systematic, clear and specific.

2. *Satisfaction of Psychological Needs of Children.* A definite curriculum helps in satisfying the psychological needs of the pupils. Man is such an animal who takes interest in purposeful activities which satisfy his present needs and prospects improve for the satisfaction of his future needs. Curriculum is framed keeping these three things in mind, and so the children take interest in carrying it out.

3. Best use of Time and Energy. When the scope of the curriculum is deemed, the teacher comes to know what he has to teach and the pupils know what they have to learn. It help in making a good use of time and energy.

4. Helps in Writing Text-books Written. A definite curriculum directs various writers to write books. While preparing the text-books the writer includes only necessary and relevant material.

5. Uniform Level of Education. A definite curriculum keeps the level of education of society uniform. Their outcome, offer us correct direction for reform in education. A definite curriculum offers facilities in keeping the level of education uniform.

6. Evaluation. It becomes easy to evaluate children with the help of the curriculum. For a specific level, after the curriculum is framed, it becomes easier to evaluate the pupils. If there is no curriculum for a particular level, then how the teacher will evaluate the abilities of the pupils.

7. Achievements of Aims of Education. Curriculum is framed for achieving the goals of education. If there is no definite curriculum before us we cannot know through what knowledge of subjects and training of activities, we are achieving the goals and which activities are useful and which are not.

BASES OF CURRICULUM

Curriculum construction should proceed keeping in view the various bases, as stated below:

1. Psychological Base. Accordingly, there should be variety in the curriculum so that the child may be able to receive education, according to his interests, aptitudes, traits and needs. On this basis, the curriculum happens to be child centred. The learning material should be assigned place in it, in accordance with their interests, aptitudes, needs, capabilities etc.

2. Sociological Base. The curriculum is framed keeping in mind the social needs, demands, assumptions, aspirations etc. From this point of view the curriculum assigns place to those activities and experiences so as to develop in pupils, sociality, cooperative feelings which are helpful in developing social character. Dewey has given importance to this base. According to him, education of the individual begins by participating in social consciousness. Keeping this principle in mind he assigned place in the curriculum to those experiences and activities only which represent social life and its activities.

3. Philosophical Base. Philosophical thoughts have considerable bearing on curriculum, since philosophy determines, the goals and assumptions of education and the curriculum is the means to achieve these goals. So, the curriculum should be framed according to the aims of education. For example, according to idealistic school, the chief aim of education is self-realisation. For achieving these aims, the idealistic curriculum assigns place to ultimate values—Truth, Beauty and Goodness.

4. Scientific Base. It is a gift of Herbert Spencer. He advocated, giving liberal education through medium of sciences. He set 'preparing for complete living' as the aim of education. To achieve this aim he gave important place to natural/physical sciences in the curriculum.

PRINCIPLES WHILE SELECTING SUBJECT-MATTER OF SOCIAL STUDIES

The scope of the subject is very vast. So, whatever is to be taught must be carefully selected to help students develop major ideas, skills, attitudes and habits for making education good for producing useful citizens. Subject-matter is not to be selected arbitrarily but it should be selected out of regard of its social relevance. Social relevance and cultural implications are not to be neglected. Social Study is the study of society. We have to train individual for their social life. Emphasis should be on the present and not on the past or remote future. One should not think that Social Studies is a mere combination of history, geography, economics and civics of course, this subject derives a lot from these, but only such events of the past, only those features of earth's surface and those ideas of social organisation are taken, which have a clear, traceable and remarkable relation with the present and daily life. In fact, while selecting matter we should be guided by our aims of Social Studies. These are two general principles which will influence our choice of subject-matter *i.e.* (1) Phychological and (2) Sociological.

Following principles may be followed for the construction of Social Studies curriculum:

1. Motivation. It should motivate the children. It should be suited to the age and needs of the child. Activities selected for adolescents should be able to stimulate adolescent response.

2. Relevance to Pupil's Experience. Old curriculum is not only vicarious experience but it was beyond the comprehension of the child and must transcend his experience if it is to be truly educative.

3. Adapted to the Maturity of the Pupil. It should be adapted to the stage of physical and mental development reached by the children. For selection and treatment of the subject-matter, we must keep in mind the age and grade. It must make an appeal to the sense of wonder or romance in the earlier years. At the secondary stage, it should be of practical utility. It would be more appreciated if it contains generalisations, wonder, practical utility and attempts at generalisations should enliven teaching.

4. Reality of Learning Situations. The situations in education must be direct experience, no doubt, adult experiences shall also be necessary. All experiences, must be from the living world and only then knowledge can be comprehensible to the children. Observing a factory, visiting a town, investigating a real social problem or reading an actual document of early period are the examples of direct learning situations.

5. Integrated Study. There should be vertical and horizontal articulation in the programme of Social Studies. A year's course should be a continuation of the previous year's work and also it should serve as the basis for the subsequent work. So curriculum should be correlated and coordinated one.

6. Adaptation to Individual Differences. Young people, no doubt, have certain common characteristics, share certain common needs, impulses and interests, but at the same time they equally differ from one another in taste, preference, skills, experience and understanding, as well as in sex and mental ability. The curriculum must be so as to meet the needs of individual differences and variations.

7. Self-Integrated Learning. Knowledge may be such as can cause self-integrated learning. Whatever new a child learns must become an integral part of his previous knowledge.

8. Adaptation to Community Characteristics. The family and the community are the first source of knowledge and interest in social studies as community is the laboratory where experiments and observations can be made. The students should get first hand knowledge of their land, people and their occupations and their modes of recreation. It should continue to extend its scope from the locality to the community at large. Both urban and rural pupils should get the chances of knowing each other.

9. Cultivation of a Critical Sense. It means that its study should train the students to see, observe and examine things clearly, looking from all view points, *i.e.* accurate observation and resisting suggestions. We should cultivate objective attitude in the minds of the children.

10. Promotion of Inter-communal Understanding. India is a museum of religions and society in our country is segmented into religious and language groups. This has adversely affected the unity and national spirit of our country. So curriculum should be such as is able to bridge the gulf between the various religions and language groups. This is the most urgent need of the hour. This can be realised by offering the child to learn some appreciation of different cultures and faiths of other groups.

11. Comprehensiveness. The course of study must be comprehensive, including a wide range of social experiences, direct and indirect which are essential for achieving the aims and objectives of Social Studies.

12. Flexibility. Curriculum is meant for pupils and pupils are different in aptitude, interest and intelligence. The experiences available out of these activities should be anticipated.

13. Right Ideals and Loyalties. Our actions are determined by the ideals we have before us. Curriculum should promote right ideals and loyalties. "In order to raise the child from the level of individual egoism and family selfishness and liberate his potentialities, every effort should be made to create in the child a sense of community first in the class, then in the successive larger groups comprised by the school, the neighbourhood, and the nation, in the progression a loyalties which will enable him later to reach the climax of membership in the world community."

14. Study of Current Affairs. Current affairs are very important for any student of Social Studies and a weekly or fortnightly review of current affairs fits in well with the social studies course. Not only they need to understand and comprehend the local and world events intelligently, they should also be trained to discriminate in the reading of newspaper and periodicals. Test of effectiveness of local education is the ability of young citizens to evaluate currents and to gauge the reliability of channels of informative.

SOCIAL STUDIES AS A CORE SUBJECT

An average normal seeks to live a democratic life, with satisfaction to himself and to his society. He has to act as a home-member, as a worker and as a citizen in society. Education is the chief and the best means for realizing these aims of life. Its outstanding function is "preparation for life". It enables a man to live as a self-sufficient, useful and healthy individual. It fits him to live as a home-member, a worker and a citizen. It enables a person to live all these lives efficiently and effectively. A functional content of education is essential to give the understanding of the environment and the way of successful functioning in it. It explains the inter-relatedness of things with the historical background. Functional content of education creates a sense of values in life, and formulates desirable patterns of attitudes and behaviour. It creates love of life and confidence in mankind.

Reasons for Making Social Studies a Core Subject

Social Studies is a core subject drawing functional material from various subject fields. Its subject-matter is "Man and his Environment". It is to be taught as a compulsory subject upto the secondary school stage because this is the final stage of education for the majority of students. Following are the reasons for making Social Studies, a core subject in schools.

1. Psychological Reasons

(i) ***Importance of Environment.*** According to psychology man is the creation of environment and his personality is best developed in an environment while human being responds to his environment he also seeks to understand it thoroughly and interpret it correctly. In small inter-personal relationships are established by means of direct participation of men in the environment. In our complex society home and other social institutions have ceased to provide the necessary training to children. This burden has now been

shifted to schools. Among all school subjects, Social Studies is the only subject which studies man and his relationship with his environment. Hence, its importance is as a core subject.

(ii) ***Importance of Behaviour.*** Psychology is the science of behaviour. In the modern age of psychology our problems are tackled better due to psychological findings. If one is psychologically convinced that he is to live along with others he requires a particular type of behaviour to interact and understand the interaction of others. This can be achieved through a course, rooted in children's day to day experiences.

2. Educational Reasons. The social, economic and political problems of the modern world are so intricate that if left to themselves or to their home and community few young men and women can be trusted to pick up the necessary information. Education has three main aims—the material, the cultural and the social.

(i) ***Material Aim.*** The parents want that education should fit the child to earn his living. They, therefore, think of education as primarily a form of vocational preparation.

(ii) ***Cultural Aim.*** The philosopher insists on cultural rather than the utilitarian aim of education. His idea of education is that it should aim at complete and harmonious development of all the capacities of the individual.

(iii) ***Social Aim.*** Both these aims ignore the important fact that a child has to play as a member of the society in which he is born.

According to the democratic idea of the modern time each citizen should take his part in decisions of national and international importance. Therefore, education must make a real contribution towards the development of the child in a social context by providing experiences which should enable the child to understand his own nature, the nature of his physical and social environment and his place within that environment. Education must develop the attitude and skills essential for group life and civic efficiency such as social mindedness truthfulness, honesty, loyalty, tolerance and co-operation etc. A modern teacher has at his command such as the new tools the wireless, the cinema, the visual aids of all types, the project method and the activity methods. All these must be set in the framework of an integrated course of study realise their full value. This brings us to the problem of the integration of subject units which is the content of Social Studies.

3. Sociological Reasons

(i) ***Development of Social Character.*** The purpose of Social Studies in schools is the development of social character. This may be done by drawing the child into the community and making him aware of its collective life and ideals.

(ii) ***Social Awareness.*** Social awareness is most essential to avoid anti-social behaviour. It gives to the child a sense of belonging, to the family, the neighbourhood, the community, the nation and humanity.

(iii) ***Socialisation if Education has Got any Aim Like Socialisation.*** Social Studies is a subject which promises to contribute much to education. This is the best fulfilled by Social Studies because Social Studies keeps this aim in the forefront.

(iv) ***Study of Society.*** In Social Studies, we study the nature of society, its present shape and how its evolution to its present form. Achievements of the society in the past and their effect on the present, is an important content of Social Studies.

(v) ***Changes and Problems.*** Social studies find out how man has changed his physical environment and adjusted himself according to his environment. This will help in produce on well-adjusted citizens prepared to solve the pressing problems of our times. It will enable our students to become efficient and effective members of the world-community.

4. Practical Reasons

(i) ***Practical Attitudes and Ideals.*** Social Studies inculcates the attitude and ideals which make one more successful in his practical life than otherwise. Our present-day life demands from us more knowledge of social behaviour and greater social awareness. Therefore, Social Studies must be taught as compulsory subject to future citizens to produce well-informed and enlightened citizens who may promote common welfare after subordinating their own selfishness and greed.

(ii) ***Re-adjustment in Nuclear Family.*** In old days there were joint families including not only mother, father and their own children, but also grand parents aunts, uncles, cousins and other members who lived under the same roof. Joint family it gave stability and security to home life. The family lived, played and worked together, depending upon each member for his contribution towards the welfare of the group. Home life is now quite different from what it was. The rapid movements of rural population towards industrial towns and the enormous increase in prices have created many social problems directly concerned with the social life of children. All this makes the content of a Social Studies course.

(iii) ***Increasing Responsibility of Citizenship.*** Since the earliest period of Indian history one of the major aims of education has been to train our children for responsible citizenship. With the establishment of democracy as a system of Government in India this aim has come into the fore-front. The task of schools in general and social studies in particular, has become increasingly greater (or the realisation of this aim.

(iv) ***Rapid Growth in Communication and Transportation.*** During the last few decades the rapid growth in communication and transportation has created a number of exceedingly complex problems in human relationships on

international level. Man-made barriers of cultural differences, colonial and commercial rivalries and intolerance etc. along with physical barriers of mountains, oceans and deserts etc. have been removed. Today, there is a free flow of ideas, communications, information and interaction among the peoples of the world.

(v) ***Increasing Responsibility for Democratic Living.*** Today, Democracy has been accepted as a way of life by a majority of the nations of the world. This has increased the personal responsibility of each citizen. Who must have a sound understanding of his or her relationship and responsibility to the group. In return, the group should also understand its responsibility to the individual. Therefore, the school should provide experiences to children which may familiarise them with democratic living and with deep appreciation of the liberty, enjoyed by the citizens of a nation. This is taught effectively through Social Studies.

(vi) ***Overcoming the Current Forces.*** Today, industrial and technological advances are making social interaction very complex and complicated. We need to understand social phenomena and the laws of change much more than before because every adult citizen is expected to participate in controlling them. This is done by the teaching of Social Studies.

(vii) ***Need of International Understanding.*** Modern man is overpowered by fear and insecurity which cannot be removed unless he has faith in the basic goodness of man. As M.K. Gandhi said "This world, this vale of sorrow which was sleeped in hatred and violence was doomed, unless the lessons of love, truth and non-violence could find their way into the home is well as the school and thereby, eventually into the social, political and economic organizations of the world. If we want to change the world, we cannot do so merely by trying to change the outside world, we must also change the world within the

world of man's mind and emotions, where the seeds of violence and hatred or peace and love, are initially sown." This is the basic educational challenge of the modern age. Today we need cooperation among nations, charity amongst groups, love amongst individuals and justice for all. Co-operation, charity and love were preached and practised by men like Plato, Buddha, Jesus Christ, Mohammed, Lincoln and Gandhi Ji. Today, these have to be woven into the fabric of our educational thought and practice so that men learn to live together, to love and respect one another, to share one another's joys and sorrows and to help one another to overcome the hurdles of life.

AS CORE SUBJECT IN INDIAN EDUCATION

1. Education for Citizenship. According to Cyril Burt, "In the relatively simple conditions that obtained down to the middle of the nineteenth century, education for citizenship could be left largely to take care of itself the social, economic and political problems of the modern world are so intricate that few young people can be trusted to pick up the necessary information, or to teach themselves to think clearly and logically on the numerous problems that confront them a well-designed and well-conducted course of social studies can fulfil the main educational requirements of a field of study. It will satisfy the need of the child to understand his environment and his relations with it and it will go far to satisfy the need of society for well-adjusted citizens prepared to participate in solving the pressing problems of our times.....

2. Education For Democracy. Today, India has accepted democracy as its form of government. Well-informed and enlightened citizenry is the first requirement for successful and first-rate working of democracy. Our new generation needs to know and understand the meaning and implications of democracy. Children of today need to be taught democracy. Only teaching of Social Studies can do this job well. It can give training to the pupils to subordinate their self-shyness to promote common good: It can prepare them for living in a democratically governed country.

3. Cultural Crisis. Today, the world is passing through a culture crisis. Never in human history was man so over-powered by fear and insecurity. Today, we need cooperation among nations, charity amongst groups, love amongst individuals and justice for all. These ideas should be woven into the fabric of educational thought and practice, so that these can be grasped by the citizens of tomorrow. This can best be achieved by social studies.

4. Practical Interdependence. Today it has become impossible for man to live in splendid isolation. Never before did the work of an individual affect the welfare of others on such a wide scale. Modern conditions of production and exchange of commodities have made the whole world one. There is an interdependence quietly and persistently operating in the activity of every farmer, manufacturer, labourer and merchant, in every part of the civilized globe. Along with physical barriers of mountains, oceans and deserts artificial barriers of cultural differences, colonial find commercial rivalries are being removed. As there is a free flow of ideas and information, there is a demand that all items of instruction should be seen and appreciated in their bearing upon the net-work of social activities. Today, the accumulation of information apart from its social bearings is worse than futile. Social Studies should be taught to every child to link learning with life.

A CRITICAL STUDY OF CURRICULUM FOR PRIMARY, MIDDLE AND HIGH CLASSES

1. Democracy and its Success. For the success of our democracy, it is imperative that our schools should gear themselves up to meet the new demands on them. These demands are nothing short of fitting the new generation of Indian to meet the new ideals and aspirations of a developing country. The secondary education, which would be the end of all formal education for the majority of the citizens must assume the responsibility of providing the necessary training for the purpose. It is with this objective that we have reconstructed our secondary school curriculum. And one great change that we have brought in it is the inclusion of Social Studies as one of the core subjects. Citizenship in a democracy is a very exacting and challenging responsibility for which every Citizen has to be carefully trained.

2. To Make the Knowledge of Social Sciences Functional. So far we have been teaching history, geography, economics and civics separately. Unfortunately all subjects have been taught in isolation as mere information subjects. But education is said to be effective only when facts become faculty and information ripens into wisdom and effective behaviour. In order to shift the emphasis of educational process from more knowledge to behaviour and the order to make the above mentioned social sciences functional in a real sense, attempt has been made to give an integrated course in the form of Social Studies. It is a study where subject-matter explains man and his relationships with environments—cultural, physical, social, economic, etc. Lopsided approach to the study of history, geography, civics does not serve any useful purpose in this present age of varied relationships. We need to develop synthetic outlook of man. A child in order to head a successful life has to study, understand and interpret his relationship to his surroundings. This is possible through an integrated approach such as social-studies.

3. To Explain about Social Environment. The entry of this subject into the schools is mainly due to the fact that history, geography, civics and economics impart formal education. They failed to explain the social environment in a comprehensive manner. But Social Studies is more concerned with life situation than with formal studies.

4. To Prepare a Child for Successful and Effective Living. It has been the accepted purpose of education to prepare a child for successful and effective living. Social Studies, dealing exclusively with man's problems, becomes essential in any programme of education which aims to preserve known values and to achieve new heights of social relationships. In no other area of educational programme it is possible to provide experiences which express and interpret life as effectively as in Social Studies. Looking from this angle Social Studies holds a key position in our school curriculum.

5. Social Studies is Education Through Life. Social Studies is also education through life. It is more to be lived and experienced than to be learnt. In Social Studies the emphasis is on the child rather than on the subject and on how he knows rather than on what he knows. It is both activity-oriented and child-centred. For a large majority of students, secondary education marks the completion of their formal education and therefore, it should be viewed primarily as a stage complete-in itself. Social Studies being the core subject provides potentialities for anticipated future development of the balanced personality of the child.

6. It Develops Attitudes, Skills and Independent Thinking. Social Studies is concerned with the development of attitudes, interests, critical and independent thinking and social sensitivity in addition to acquisition of skill and information. In his way, it develops the whole personality.

SOCIAL STUDIES AS CORE SUBJECT

There are various social sciences which are being taught in schools. Their separate material has made it difficult for the pupils to understand social events in their totality. The pupils are able to collect facts but they are not able to understand their relationship to real life situations. Therefore, technique of correlation, integration or even fusion has made the knowledge of social science as unified in the shape of social studies.

Fusion. Fusion is a merged content of two or three subjects such as fusion of civics, history and geography. In this synthesis the subjects disappear completely. For the past several years there has been a steady movement against the teaching of separate social subjects like, geography, history, civics and economics, etc., at the secondary stage. In their place, a unified approach is commended to be achieved through the fusion of elements from various social sciences into single broad programme. This programme is built around a series of broad topics which are intended to introduce the young child to his physical and social environment. However, some people argue that many sidedness of the social studies course is confusing for the students. Why should not we teach history, geography, civics, economics, literature, etc. separately at the secondary stage? We can expect from these subjects the same social concepts and skills as we expect from the study of Social Studies. These people do not understand that knowledge given in isolation, especially to school children .cannot be easily understood and grasped by them. Children take less interest if they are offered discriminated ideas in social sciences. For this unified course of Social Studies is preferable to separate subjects.

Integration. In integration, the subjects remain but the boundaries between them are more or less overlooked in arranging materials for teaching purposes. The subject content is kept intact, but the walls of their compartments yield to allow a passage back and forth. Integration is achieved by teaching units.

The aim of education, upto secondary school stage is to give only general or liberal education. For majority of the children, it is the final or conclusive stage of education. We have, therefore widen their vision and out-look on life as a whole, so as to enable them to play their effective part as useful and enlightened citizens. This is possible only through an integrated course of social studies which not only include the knowledge of physical, cultural, economic, social and civic experience of man but also the development of attitudes and skills.

Correlation. Correlation is inter-relation of various social sciences. If a teacher is well informed in various social sciences and their contents and if he is good at working out similarities, differences and relationships, he is then likely to be able to workout a good relation. But the, real purpose of correlation is to let each social science contribute to the value of other subjects. Correlation is a process a way of thinking in which learning becomes more meaningful and effective Thus, the term 'Correlation' denotes the relationships between various subjects, *e.g.* history with geography and history with civics.

Separate subjects like history, geography civics, economics, etc. suffer from many limitations. In history, we have so far been emphasising individuals and their performances, during various periods in the past. Contemporary world and its issues could not be understood and explained by this subject. Similarly geography when taught in isolation described only boundaries, and locations and discussed mountains, oceans and rivers without explaining their effect upon human life. Civics dealt only with the structure and functions of government and not the activities and functions of government and not the activities and functions of various social groups like the school, the family, the local community, etc. Similarly economics has been emphasising only abstract theories and definitions and the ethics of earning and using wealth. It did not explain the social nature of economic activity. We must start with the present day life of man and see how far he has learnt to control or he is controlled by physical environment and how far he has been successful in adapting himself to various occupations and various social situations. This is possible only through it unified course of Social Studies.

ROLE OF SCHOOL

Community versus Social Education. Family of the child and his community gave him all the social education that he required because community life in those days was quite simple. But various scientific inventions, developed means of communication and transport have made the community life very complex. Home has ceased to create that awareness of relationship of various social institutions. So this function of home and community has also become, the obligation of the school. Now school has to provide what home and community provided in the past. "It has, to provide total education—education for knowledge for background, for standards, for awareness skill, for understanding, for culture, for making a contribution, for sense of belonging, for attitudes and for a proper orientation to the modern world". All this can be attained through a well-planned course of Social Studies.

Social Studies are Helpful in Specialisation. A good background of Social Studies, at the secondary stage is helpful to prepare a ground for specialisation in different subjects at higher stages of learning. It will lay a good foundation on which the superstructions of specialisation can safety be built it is, therefore, that a composite course of social studies is more useful than the teaching of history, geography, civics, economics, current affairs, etc., as separate subjects, at the secondary school stage.

It is quite common to use Social Sciences and Social Studies as synonyms. But, there is a great difference between the two. Social sciences deal with detailed, systematic and logical study of human relationship. They maintain a certain standard of scholarship. They are storehouses of knowledge and source of scientific social findings. They are concerned with research, investigation, discovery and experimentation. Social sciences are always eager to expand the boundaries of human knowledge.

In contrast with Social sciences, Social Studies material is primarily designed for instructional purposes in school. Social Studies consist of those portion of social sciences which have been selected and adopted for use in schools. Thus, Social Studies, is the simplified and, re-organised format social sciences. It deals with human relationship which can be understood at school level. This shows that the two differ only in level of difficulty and not in kind. As compared to Social science. Social Studies must be simple, easy, appealing, interesting and learnable. Social sciences are the theory part of human affairs while social studies is the practice part. This distinction can easily be seen in the case of political science and civics. While political science is an advanced, scholarly subject, taught and studied at the graduate level Civics is a simplified version of political science, meant for children in schools.

PATEL COMMITTEE CURRICULUM OF SOCIAL STUDIES

ENVIRONMENTAL STUDIES

CLASSES I AND II

1. ***Our Family.*** Life, structure and functions.
2. ***Our Home.*** Shelter, facilities, love.
3. ***Our Neighbourhood.*** Life, work, cleanliness, space.

4. ***Our Earth.*** Features, vegetation, water, minerals.
5. ***Our Sky.*** Light, heat, weather, stars.
6. ***Man's Life.*** Interesting imaginative stories.

CLASS III

Section A

1. ***The World We Live In.*** Continents, oceans, our country in the world.
2. ***Life in the District.*** Setting, occupation, festivals.
3. ***Life in our States.*** Location, relief, vegetation, resources, occupations, communications.
4. ***Life in our Country.*** Food, clothing, occupations languages, festivals.
5. ***Institutions which Help us.*** Panchayat, cooperatives, health centres, education, transport.
6. ***Our Heritage.*** Stories of great men and women, and of early men.

Section B

7. ***The Earth and the Sky.*** Day and nigbt, heavenly bodies.
8. ***The Weather.*** Influence in our lives, soils and crops.

CLASS IV

Section A

1. ***India—Physical Divisions.*** Mountains, plains, rivers and plateaus.
2. ***India—Resources.*** Human and natural (soil, water, minerals).
3. ***India—Transport and Communications.*** On land, water and air, post and telegraph and telephone.
4. ***The People of India.*** National symbols and festivals, one country.
5. ***Indian Heritage I.*** Monuments, music, dances, religions, scripts, languages, handicrafts, festivals.

6. ***Indian Heritage II.*** Stories of famous rulers, reformers, writers, scientists, saints.

7. ***Our Freedom Struggle.*** Briefly through some of the more prominent leaders.

Section B

8. ***Earth and Sky.*** Planet around the Sun, Revolution of the earth on tilted axis.

9. ***Air, Water and Weather.*** Seasons affect the lives of the people, plants and animals, importance of clear water.

10. ***Soil Erosion and Conservation.*** Wind, kinds of soil, and ways to conserve soil.

CLASS V

Section A

1. ***The Globe and Map of the World.*** Hemispheres, Equator, Poles, Tropics, Arctic circles.

2. ***India and Neighbouring Countries.*** Many ways of living life and occupations in some distinctive areas of the world, *e.g.* Tundra, Savannah, Desert, Equatorial Mediterranean.

3. ***Our Shrinking World.*** Transport and communications, land, sea, air, radio, television, newspapers, cinema and satellites.

4. ***How we Govern Ourselves.*** The state and central governments, fundamental rights, directive principles, duties of a citizen.

5. ***The United Nations.*** Cooperation among nations, work of UNICEF, WHO, UNESCO, India in the U.N.

6. ***The Changing World.*** Stories of scripts, numbers, trade, money.

7. ***Discoveries and Scientists.*** Columbus, Galileo, Newton, Einstein.

8. ***Great Men.*** Socrates, Lincoln, Lenin, Tolstoy, Mahatma Gandhi.

Section B

9. ***The Earth and the Sky.*** National and artificial satellites shadows.

10. ***Air and Water.*** Air pressure, composition of air-pollution of air, water a good solvent, purification of water.

11. ***Natural Resources.*** Rocks, minerals, coal, petroleum, soils.

HISTORY

Class VI-Ancient India

1. ***Pre-history.*** Man as a nomad—discovery and use of metals, invention of the wheel-Framing.

2. ***The Harappan Culture.*** Cities-occupations-religious Script.

3. ***Life in the Vedic Age.*** Settlements—Economic and political life—Religion.

4. ***Rise of Magadha.*** Kingdoms and republics-emergence of towns—Jainism and Buddhism.

5. ***The Mauryan Empire.*** Persian and Greek invasions-Chandragupta Maurya Ashoka administration.

6. ***India from 200 B.C. to A.D. 300.*** Satavahanas-Cholas-Pandyas Cheras Shakas Khushaṇs.

7. ***The Age of the Guptas.*** Administration trade religion art and science.

8. ***India from A.D. 500 to A.D. 800.*** Harsha—The Deccan and South India-Art and architecture.

9. ***India and the World.*** Rise of Islam-The Arabs in India-India's contacts with other countries.

Class VII-Medieval India

1. ***India from A.D. 800 to A.D. 1200.*** Kingdom of South-Religion-Architecture-The struggle for Kannauj-Turkish Invasions-Religion-Art and architecture.

2. ***The Sultanate of Delhi.*** Mamluks-Khaljis-Tughlaks-The Bahmani and Vijaynagar Kingdoms-Sufi and Bhakti Movements.
3. ***The Advent of the Mughals and the Europeans.*** Kingdoms in the Deccan-Renaissance in Europe-Voyages of discovery.
4. ***The Mughal Empire.*** Akbar-Jahangir and Shahjahan-Aurangzeb—Rise of the Marathas—Art-Architecture-Literature.
5. ***Decline of the Mughal Empire.*** Invasions-Rise of Independent states.

Class VIII-Modern India

1. ***India in the Eighteenth Century.*** Expansion of the Maratha Power-Society and Polity.
2. ***The Rise and Growth of British Empire in India.*** The Carnatic wars-the British conquest of Bengal-British paramountcy.
3. ***Administrative Structure of the British Empire in India.*** Civil, Judicial- Revenue system.
4. ***Impact of British Rule on Indian Economy and Society upto 1875.*** The village economy-industry and trade-educational and Social reform.
5. ***The Revolt of 1857.*** Cause-nature-results.
6. ***Reorganization of the British Empire in India.*** The Act of 1858-Civil services-policy of 'Divide and Rule.'
7. ***Changes in Economy and Society After 1858.*** Agriculture and railways-plantations-industries-economic conditions. Social life: Education-social and religious reform movements-cultural awakening.
8. ***Rise of Indian Nationalism and the Struggle for Freedom.*** The Indian National Congress-Partition of Bengal-The Gandhian Era- Civil Disobedience-The I.N.A.-Quit India Movement.
9. ***Achievement of Independence.*** Immediate Problems.

ClassVII-Our Constitution

1. ***Chief Features of our Constitution.*** Basic Principles, National Government-state government-rights-duties-directive principles-national symbols.
2. ***Law-Making Process.*** Parliament-State legislature, How Laws are made.
3. ***Executing Laws.*** President-Prime Minister and the council of ministers, governor-chief minister and the council of ministers, public services.
4. ***Interpreting Law.*** Supreme Court, High Courts and subordinate courts.
5. ***Project Work***

Class VIII-Independent India—Achievements and Challenge

1. ***Our National Goals.*** Democracy-Socialism and Secularism, International Cooperation.
2. ***Strengthening our Democracy.*** Citizenship in a democracy-Literacy in India.
3. ***Social and Economic Reconstruction.*** Poverty-population-unemployment casteism.
4. ***Five Year Plans Achievements and Failures.*** Agriculture, industries-rural life.
5. ***Defence of the Country: Armed Forces.*** Territorial army-Border Securiry Forces-N.C.C., AC.C., citizens and defence.
6. ***India and the World.*** Need for cooperation-co-existence, the United Nations.
7. ***Project Work.***

GEOGRAPHY

Class VI

1. ***The Earth as a Globe.*** Distance and direction on a map. The earth and the solar system-rotation and revolution-latitude and longitude.

2. ***Africa-Land and People.*** Land, climate, vegetation and wild life, equatorial lands-Savanna lands-Sahara lands-the Veld and the Mediterranean lands.

3. ***Asia-Land and People.*** Land, climate, vegetation and wild life, the people. Pakistan, Nepal, Bhutan, Bangladesh, Burma and Sri Lanka.

Class VII

1. ***Atmosphere and Hydrosphere.*** Air-temperature-pressure and wmds.

2. ***Australia-Land and People.*** Land, climate, vegetation and wild life, the people.

3. ***South America-Land and People.*** Land, climate, vegetation an wild life, the people.

4. ***North America.*** Land and People-Land, Climate, Vegetation and Wild life-the people-Canada-the United States.

5. ***Practical Work.*** Observation and keeping records of sunrise and sunset. Stars and constellations studying local maps, landforms in the neighbourhood.

Class VIII

1. ***Lithosphere and Landforms.*** The crus of the earth-rocks.

2. ***Europe-Land and People.*** Land, Climate, Vegetation and Wild life-the people-France, the United Kingdom and Germany.

3. ***The Soviet Union-Land and People.*** Land, Climate, Vegetation and Wild life, the people.

4. ***India—Physical Setting.*** Relief Climate, Vegetation, Wild life.

5. ***India—Its Agricultural Resources.*** Soil-lrrigation-crops-methods of farming.

6. ***India—Minerals and Industries.*** Iron, coal, petroleum, bauxite, manganese, textiles, sugar; oil refinery, heavy industries, small scale and cottage industries.

7. ***India—Trade, Transport and Population.*** Internal and external, land, water and air, population-distribution and density.
8. ***Practical Work—Weather Study.*** Today, weather, observation and recording.

CIVICS

1. Man as a social being.
2. Man as a citizen.
3. Local self-government.
4. State and national government.
5. Rights and duties of a citizen.
6. Democracy in India.
7. India as a nation: unity in diversity.
8. Social and economic challenges before the country.
9. India and the world.
10. India and the United Nations.
11. Project work.

GEOGRAPHY

General Geography of the World with Special Reference to India

1. ***Landforms.*** Continents, mountains, plateaus, plains, landforms in India.
2. ***Climate.*** Climate zones, in the world and in India.
3. ***Natural Regions of the World.*** Tropical, temperate, cold lands.
4. ***Natural Resources.*** Soil; vegetation, animals, minerals and water in world and in India.
5. ***Major Occupations.*** Primitive, pastoral, agricultural, industrial.
6. ***Agriculture.*** Principal agricultural areas, crops and practices in the world and in India.

7. ***Minerals and Power.*** Major minerals and mining areas, water and nuclear power.
8. ***Industries.*** Important areas and location, heavy and light industries, production and output.
9. ***Transport and Communication.*** Land, water, air.
10. ***International Trade.*** Commodities, import-export, foreign changes.
11. ***Population of the World and India.*** Distribution, density, control of population.
12. ***Case Studies.*** Life of the people in various parts of the world and in India.

SOCIAL SCIENCE SYLLABUS PRESCRIBED BY N.C.E.R.T.

UPPER PRIMARY OR MIDDLE CLASSES

HISTORY

Class VI-Ancient India

Unit I...... (a) How and Why We Study the Past.

(b) Geographical and Ethnographical Features of India.

(c) Pre-historic Culture of India.

Unit II......The Harappa Culture.

Unit III.....New Cultural Patterns in India (1500 B.C. to 600 B.C.).

Unit IV.....India from the Rise of Magadha to the Mauryan Empire.

Unit V......India during the Period 200 B.C. to 300 AD.

Unit VI.....India from 300 AD to 800 AD.

Class VII-Medieval India

Unit I.....India and the World.

Unit II....India from 800 AD. to 1200 AD.

Unit III...India from early 13th to early 16th century.

Unit IV....Advent of the Mughals and Europeans.

Unit V.....India under the Mughals.

Unit VI....Disintegration of the Mughal Empire.

Class VIII-Modern India

Unit I.....India and the Modern World.

Unit II.....The Rise, Growth and Impact of British Rule in India.

Unit III....Revolts against British Rule.

Unit IV.....British Policies and Administration in India after 1858.

Unit V......Changes in Economy and Society.

Unit VI.....Rise of Indian Nationalism and Struggle for Freedom, upto Independence.

GEOGRAPHY

Class VI

Unit I.....The Earth—Our Planet.

Unit II....Africa—Lands and People.

Unit III....South America—Lands and People.

Unit IV....Australia—Lands and People.

Unit V.....Antarctica—Land, Climate, Natural, Vegetation and Wild Life.

Unit VI.....Practical Work—Map Reading.

Class VII

Unit I......Atmosphere and Hydrosphere

Unit II.....North America—Lands and Peoples.

Unit III.....Europe—Lands and People.

Unit IV.....The Soviet Union—Land and People.

Unit V.......Practical Work—Studying the Weather and Night-sky.

Class VIII

Unit I......Lithosphere and Land Forming.

Unit II.....Asia—Lands and People.

Unit III.....India—Physical Setting.

Unit IV.....India—Natural Resources.

Unit V.......India—Human Resources.

Unit VI......India—Economic Development.

Unit VII.....Practical Work—Studying Local Maps.

CIVICS

Class VI

Unit I......Civic Life in Community Development of the Community.

Unit II.....Local Government Rural.

Unit III.....Local Government Urban.

Unit IV.....District Administration.

Unit V.......Preservation of Property of the Community.

Unit VI......Project Work.

Class VII-Our Constitution

Unit I......Features of Our Constitution.

Unit II......Law Making Process.

Unit III.....Executing Laws.

Unit IV......Interpreting Laws.

Unit V........Project Work.

Class VIII-Independent India—Achievements and Challenges

Unit I......Our National Goals.

Unit II.....Strengthening the Democracy.

Unit III....Our Social Problems.

Unit IV....Our Economic Problems.

Unit V.......National Integration.

Unit VI......Defence of the Country.

Unit VII.....India and the World.

Unit VIII....World Problems: (a) Arms Race, (b) Disparities between Developing and Developed countries, (c) Environmental Pollution.

Unit IX.......Project Work.

SECONDARY CLASSES (IX AND X)

HISTORY

Semester I

Unit I.....Preliminary Stage.

Unit II....Bronze Age Civilizations.

Unit III...Early Iron Age Societies (1200 B.C. to 600 AD.).

Unit IV....Early African and American Cultures and Civilizations.

Unit V......The Medieval World.

Semester II

Unit VI.....Beginning of the Modern Age.

Unit VII....Capitalism and the Industrial Revolution.

Unit VIII....Revolutionary and Nationalist Movements.

Unit IX.......Imperialism.

Semester III

Unit X......The First World War.

Unit XI.....The Russian Revolution.

Unit XII....The World from 1919 to the Second World War.

Unit XIII...The World after the Second World War.

Unit XIV...The Cultural Heritage of India.

Unit XV.....Indian Awakening.

Unit XVI.....India's Struggle for Freedom, upto Independence.

GEOGRAPHY

Semester I

Unit I......Map Skills.

Unit II.....Natural Environment.

Unit III....Natural Resources and their Utilization.

Semester II

Unit IV....Human Interaction with the Environment.

Semester III

Unit V.....India, Physical features, Climate, Natural Vegetation and Wild Life.

Unit VI....Natural Resources.

Semester IV

Unit VII....Developing Our Resources.

Unit VIII...Field Study Project Work.

CIVICS

Semester I

Unit I......Man as a Citizen.

Unit II.....Government at Local Level.

Unit III....Government at the State and National Levels.

Semester II

Unit IV.....India as a Nation.

Unit V.......Indian Democracy at Work.

Unit VI......Challenges Facing our Country Today.

Unit VII.....India and World Peace.

ECONOMICS

Semester I

Unit I.......Understanding an Economy.

Unit II......An Overview of the Indian Economy.

Semester II

Unit III......Infrastructure of the Indian Economy.

Unit IV......Towards Economic Development.

Unit V........State as an Agency for Economic Development.

CRITICAL OBSERVATIONS ON NCERT SYLLABUS

Advantages

In accordance with the latest demands of Indian education the syllabus in Social Sciences, prescribed by N.C.E.R.T. is a satisfactory attempt. It is based on the principle that an integrated course, while recognising the existence of its constituent subjects, fulfils the needs and interests of students, along the logical demands of subject. Therefore, that a lot of practical work have been recommended in the syllabus, while teaching the various components. It includes activities field surveys, tours and trips, map-reading and map-making, project work, collection of cartoons, newspaper cuttings and pictures, preparation of time lines, graphs and charts and maintaining a record book.

Disadvantages

1. ***Dominated by History.*** History occupies the most important place in the syllabus prescribed for various classes. The entire History of India, from pre-historic times upto the present days, has been prescribed in Middle classes. In high classes have been prescribed world history from the "Evolution of Life on Earth" upto the World after the Second World War, British Occupation of India, Indian Awakening and India's Struggle for Freedom, the study of all the ancient world civilizations, early African and American civilizations as well as the civilizations of medieval Europe, Arabia and East Asia, along with the world revolutionary movements, like the American Revolution, the French Revolution and the Russian Revolution have been included in the syllabus for high classes. Thus, covering a very long period of time and almost all the major areas of the world history syllabus is too heavy for 9th and 10th classes.
2. ***Defeating the Purpose.*** The syllabus defeats the very purpose for which social sciences have been included as a core subject. It encourages the writing of books, with separate chapters on different subjects like History, Geography, Civics and Economics. Specialist teachers of various social sciences are their teaching in the same old fashion. There is no co-ordinated teaching. As a teacher of this subject is specialist only in one, or at the most, two social sciences. So he skips while teaching over other

subjects or portions of the subjects in which he has not specialised. Thus, co-ordinated teaching is actually undertaken and pursued in this subject, with all its projects, activity programmes, group work and discussions etc.

3. ***Traditionalism.*** Traditionalism dominates the entire syllabus. Large portions of history, geography, civics and economics have been included in the syllabus under separate unit-heads. It is not a psychologic integration of material simply a combination of various subjects though according to recommendations of N.C.E.R.T. itself. "The various components, drawn from different social sciences, should not, however, be seen as isolated components, but as being interrelated." The combination of different subjects has made the syllabus lengthy and monotonous. When generally five periods a week are allotted to the teaching of social sciences, in the time table. It is not possible to finish the entire syllabus, for each class, in one academic year.

❑

4

Audio-Visual Aids in Teaching

There was a time when "Text-book" was the only device of teaching and 'lecture-method' was the only procedure in class-room. But now, the modern teacher uses a large number of visual and auditory aids to make the teaching-learning process effective and interesting. Instead of a text-book the children are now shown material which they can see, hear, feel and think about. All possible devices of sight and sound are utilized to arouse and maintain interest of the students in Social Studies. It is rightly said that one seeing is worth a hundred telling. It is, therefore, quite appropriate to use audio-visual material to aid teaching and facilitate learning of Social Studies. As senses are the gate-way of learning, beginning of teaching Social Studies should be made with teaching aids. Audio-Visual aids properly used cannot justly be regarded as supplementary learning, they are fundamental. They stimulate experiences and facilitate learning. The use of audio-visual materials is particularly effective in the class of low achievers or slow learners. They provide a simplified view of complicated data. They speak a universal language of form, colour, position and motion.

Learning is experiencing. It is primarily a sensory experience. The sensory experiences are interpreted by the individual. According to Olsen, learning experiences occur on three levels and to each level are related certain types of audio-visual materials. They are:

1. Direct Experience. It consists in having first-hand and direct sensory contact with the actual objects. This includes visits to factories, dams, mines, ports, rivers, mountains, parliaments etc. They provide first hand experiences.

2. Symbolic and Symbolic Experience. In this category, we include experiences which one has through words, oral or written. These, experiences are gained at conceptual level and students get them through the use of verbal illustrations, explanation and descriptions. Educationists are of the opinion that with a view to vitalise and facilitate the learning process in schools, more emphasis should be put on direct and representative experiences and less on symbolic ones. Though ultimately conceptional learning in our goal, yet it will be possible only when a good store of sensory experiences has been built up.

3. Representative Experience. Direct experiences are very expensive and is not within the reach of every student. It is not possible to visit various historical places, far off mountains, etc. In that case we may use such representative experiences which though less concrete, yet representatively and are, thus, very useful. We may have models, pictures, maps, charts, graphs, specimens, film strips, etc. in this category.

NEED AND IMPORTANCE OF AUDIO-VISUAL AIDS IN SOCIAL STUDIES

In Social Studies, various modern methods are there to impart all kinds of experiences, and explain and expand ideas. That is why, in order to organise and to impart full knowledge it becomes necessary to use pictures, maps, graphs and charts, etc. which represent social facts. Their use, not only helps in pupils learning, but they come to know also those things which are necessary in daily life. Through their effective use, pupils get a lot of help in understanding current events, 'Because of their use, the child is conscious every moment, to receive new ideas and under such new-situations, he acts intelligently. In Social Studies, great need is self for the development of concepts, improvement of attitudes and expansion of interests. Due to their use, pupils can properly hear lessons taught in the class, and hence become the basis for group planning, logical deliberation and collective exchange of views.

Importance. In the words of E.B.Weslley, "All audio-visual aids provide experiences. Through their use relations between words and objects are easily established. Pupils save time and with their help they come to know about simple and correct facts." These, on the one hand, amuse pupils, and on the other, pupils learn to appreciate various things. Complicated things become simple. These develop imagination power of pupils and their observation. Quite possible, that a need may arise to define such an arrangement but, it needs no translator, since in these the universal language of nature, colour, condition, pace is employed. Thus, they offer royal road far learning.

1. Senses are Gate-ways of Knowledge. Senses are considered as the gate-ways for learning. So, the experiences acquired through senses, facilitate learning. The child cannot understand new wards and unfamiliar things, till these are related to his experiences. Audio-visual aids help greatly in acquiring experiences related to senses. Small children particularly need concrete experiences. In Social Studies, direct and indirect, both types of experiences are important for which audio-visual aids prove helpful.

2. Help in Stimulating the Process of Learning. These not only accelerate learning, but they do not forget these experiences for quite long time, because of these aids pupils become curious and begin to take active part in learning process.

3. Clarity and Reality in the Learning Situation. These aids are quite interesting and inspiring. These bring clarity and concretness in the learning of the topic. These are good means of attracting and focussing attention and arousing interests on the part of the pupils.

4. Helpful in Imparting Direct Experiences. These are complementary to direct experiences. While teaching about life in the past of the remote regions, it may not be quite possible to give them direct experience. On such occasions these aids can greatly help in understanding new concepts, facts and symbols and in place of direct experiences we can very effectively use pictures, models etc. Sometimes the use of silent or talking films saves a lot of time and as compared with the knowledge directly gained, much more knowledge is acquired, in this way.

5. Useful for Slow Learners. These aids greatly help the slow learners. Such children cannot comprehend all essential things from the text-books and so they are considered backward. Such children can easily learn and assimilate new things with the help of pictures, films, models, radio etc.

6. Help in Stimulating Imagination and Thinking. The aids which impart perceptual knowledge are for more effective and explicit than the originalones. So, with their use, teaching process becomes natural and simple. The audio-visual aids stir imaginative capabilities and also develop observation, analytical and synthetical abilities. Thus aids can be highly useful in this direction.

7. Opportunities for Activities. Through the use of these aids, pupils get opportunities for doing various kinds of activities. Pupils get opportunities for discussion, after a film is shown.

8. Helpful to Attain Perfect Knowledge. It has been experimental proved that the pupils, through the proper use of aids, not only quickly learn, but they retain for longer time whatever is learnt. When pupils see, hear, touch, taste, smell, their experiences get concretised and those become stable to a considerable extent. Knowledge got with the help of pictures, models, charts or by similar aids, can be recalled at proper time. So, we can say that knowledge acquired through the use of the aids, becomes strengthened.

9. Meets Shortage of Resources. Their use removes the deficiencies of those are as of school and thereby compensates the scarcity of subject experts. For example, radio lessons by good teachers and the T.V., telecast of lessons of Social Studies are there.

10. Develop Scientific Attitude. The use of A.V aids in the class, with the systematic use of other material based on technological principles, develops scientific outlook in pupils.

In the end, the need and importance of these aids lies in creating a teaching-learning situation by putting the teacher and pupils in an environment full of life, activity, casting permanent impact. In this way, at all levels of teachers training the training in the use of audio-visual aids is important.

TYPES OF TEACHING AIDS

Basing his classification upon the kinds of experiences presented through the aids Edgar Dale calls it the "Cone of Experience." As classified by him, the range of experience through audio-visual aids is between direct experience and pure abstraction. These division overlap and sometimes blend into each other. Dale desires the cone of experience to be a 'visual metaphor' of learning experiences depicting the various items in the order of increasing abstractions as one proceeds from direct purposeful experience which is the bedrock of all education. At the second stage are used the contrivances like models.

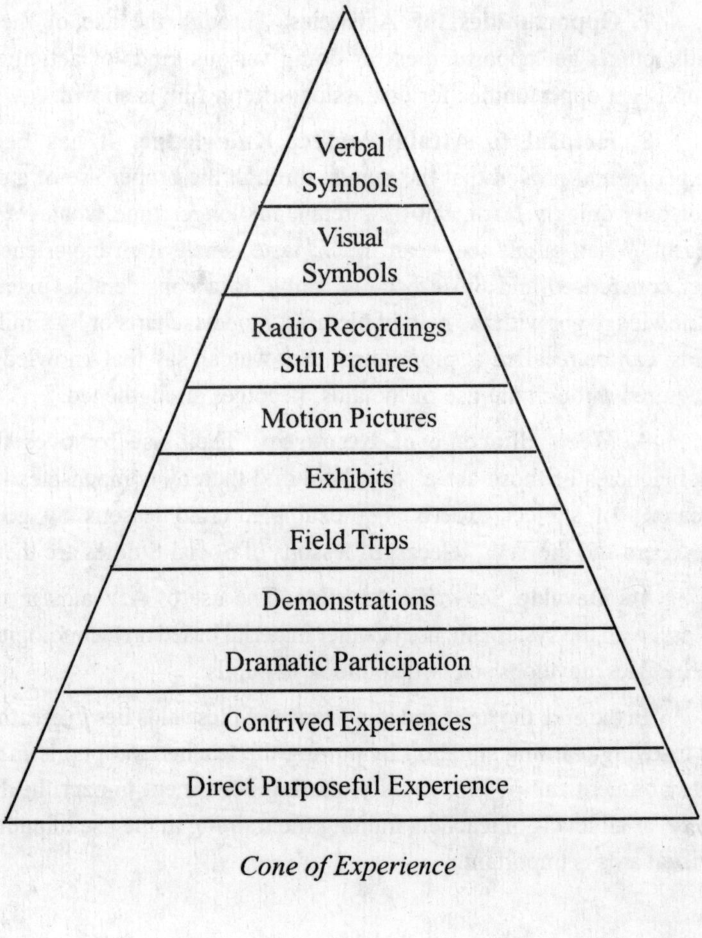

Cone of Experience

Dramatics invoke a reconstructed experience and step in where contrivances fail. Participation is better than mere watching.

As generally we cannot participate in the experience and have to be spectators. Observation, comes upper-most in education. This category includes items like demonstrations, field trips, exhibits, motion pictures, radio, recordings and pictures, in which we simply watch and listen. Teaching aids like film projectors, radio and epidiascope come in this category.

Teaching different countries we have to show them a 'map' or a 'chart' shows abstract representations of the originals. These may be included in the category of 'visual symbols'.

Types of Teaching Aids

1. ***Printed Aids***
   - *(i)* Periodicals
   - *(ii)* Books
   - *(iii)* Newspapers
2. ***Visual Aids***
   - *(i)* Slides
   - *(ii)* Film strips
   - *(iii)* Models
   - *(iv)* Graphs and Charts
   - *(v)* Pictorial materials
   - *(vi)* Globes and Maps
3. ***Audio Aids***
   - *(i)* Tape Recordings
   - *(ii)* Phonograph discs
   - *(iii)* Radio
4. ***Audio-Visual Aids***
   - *(i)* Motion Pictures
   - *(ii)* Television
   - *(iii)* Dramatisation.

What is an Audio-Visual Aid?

Audio-Visual Aids have been defined in these words: "Any device which by sight or sound increases the individual's experience, beyond that acquired through reading, may be described as an audio-visual aid to learning." It is only a means of stimulating interest at a particular time, during the course of a lesson. Audio-Visual aids are additional means to particular ends and at times contribute valuable aids to learning a situation. They arouse curiosity and interest about the extension, application and development of the topic in hand. They provoke additional mental activity. They satisfy a felt need and enrich or improve the child's understanding about a particular topic for which it has been utilized. They must be used in full context to some point in the lesson and not for the sake of entertainment aids used merely, for their entertainment value, contribute nothing to learning. These cannot be considered as teaching aids.

Advantages of Audio-Visual Aids

According to Edgar Bruce Weslley, audio-visual aids furnish experiences. They facilitate the association of objects and words. They save pupil's time and they provide simple and authentic information. They enrich and extend one's appreciation and furnish pleasant entertainment They provide a simplified view of complicated data. They stimulate the imagination and develop the pupil's power of observation. These aids may need explanation but they do not need translators. They speak a universal language of form, colour, position and motion. They constitute one of the royal roads to learning. Following are the advantages of these aids:

1. ***Provision of Sensory Experience.*** Learning requires an adequate background of sensory experience. New words and unfamiliar objects cannot be followed and understood properly unless they are attached to specific, elements of one's experience. However, both direct and indirect learning experiences are important in the teaching of Social Studies. Lessons should have a multiple sense appeal as stimuli, which appeal to more than one sense organ, are perceived and remembered easier and better.

2. ***Supplement to Direct Experience.*** Direct experiences can very well be supplemented with audio-visual aids by vicarious or representative learning visiting a post office or a cotton textile mill pupils can learn more about the postal system and about the manufacture of cloth if these direct learning experiences or followed by seeing a film or motion picture on the subject. Seeing such a film adds to the information already gained from actual visits and trips.
3. ***Provision of Substitutes for Direct Experiences.*** Audio-visual materials will come to our aid all that time to facilitate the understanding of new concepts, facts and symbols. Pictures, models and specimens etc. may be used as accurate and effective substitutes of direct learning experiences. At times the study of particular films and still pictures may be more economical saving a lot of energy and time and giving us even more knowledge of the facts or objects that is possible through direct learning experiences.
4. ***Important Motivators.*** Audio-visual aids are important motivators. They possess vividness, clarity and dramatic appeal. Children enjoy looking at pictures, going to movies and listening to the radio. These are effective medium of holding the attention and to stimulating new interests and activities among children. These motivate pupils to learn faster, remember longer, gain more accurate information and understand the delicate concepts and meanings better. Aids motivate learning as they satisfy the immediate curiosity of the child.
5. ***More Efficient Learning.*** With the proper use of audio-visual aids pupils not only learn more rapidly but they also remember the facts, thus learned, for longer period. As a child sees, hears, touches, tastes and smells, his experiences are more permanent. As mental images created by pictures, models, charts and other such aids are easy to recall more efficient learning is possible.

6. ***Effective Aid to the Slow Learner.*** Audio-visual aids are particularly helpful to poor readers and slow-learners who cannot get all the required knowledge from the text-book. They can more easily understand and remember the facts, gained through pictures, movies, models and radio etc. than gathered from abstract symbols and printed pages.

7. ***Meaningful Learning.*** Verbal descriptions of abstract things are beyond the comprehension of young children. Meaningful material is easily learned and assimilated by the child and forgotten at a slower speed. Learning involves knowledge as well as meaning of things. Rich meaning provides rich learning. Audio-visual aids break the monotony of the formal type of teaching, and provide meaning to each and everything used or displayed in the class.

8. ***Development of the Power of Imagination and Observation.*** Audio-visual aids provide sensory images much more clear and effective than the verbal images. It makes learning more natural and easy. Audio-visual aids stimulate imagination and develop the power of observation, analysis and synthesis.

Need for Audio-Visual Materials in Social Studies

The Social Studies teacher makes use of a variety of modern techniques of expression for broadening the pupil's conception of ideas and for creating more vital experience for him. Modern audio-visual material represent social facts in pictures, maps, graphs or charts. These modern devices, serve the Social Studies classroom as aids to learning. They are also a source of information which the pupil needs in daily living. Their effective use helps the pupil in developing a new approach to the understanding of current affairs. The use of such materials, increases the pupil's ability to be alert to the flood of ideas to which he is continually being subjected and to respond intelligently to all such stipule. There is a great need of using audio-visual materials for developing concepts, improving attitudes and extending appreciations and interests. By enabling pupils to see and hear what is being studied by them in the class these aids provide concrete base for group planning, critical thinking and group discussion. Appreciation of the contribution of others and improved attitudes towards other groups are developed as children learn about common needs and activities of mankind through the use of realistic audio-visual materials.

CORRECT USE OF THE AUDIO-VISUAL AIDS

1. Use when Required. Audio-visual aids should be used when and where necessary. These are not to be used just for the sake of using.

2. Treat as Means. The teacher must treat audio-visual aids as the means to an end.

3. Simple. The audio-visual aids should be simple creating only genuine interest and arousing too much of curiosity, because, otherwise their pupils' attention will be distracted and they will pay attention to the aids rather than to the lesson.

4. Preferably Grow before the Students. Generally speaking, there are occasions when it is better to draw a map, a sketch, a diagram or a graph on the black-board in front of the students.

5. Properly Exhibited. In proper exhibition a number of factors should be kept in mind for example, the teacher should not place a number of audio-visual aids before, the students. He should keep them hidden and bring out only that aid when it is required to be shown. He should see before hand that there is nail etc., on the wall to hang the picture or the chart. He should see that the, apparatus works properly. The audio-visual aids should be exhibited before the students for a sufficiently long time, so that their curiosity is satisfied, and they have properly observed what is required to be observed.

AUDIO-VISUAL AIDS

Followings are the aids of Audio-Visual used in schools:

Black Board/Chalk Board

To teach with the help of black board/chalk board is one of the oldest methods. Now in place of black board, chalk boards are being used. These, instead, of being black, may be green, yellow or of any of colour. Social Studies/Science teachers have started experiencing that chalk board can be very useful for them. Their use can be made for various points along with framing outline of any topic for drawing and sketching diagrams, figures, plans to develop and to write summary. Since black board is the cheapest and easily available, its proper utilisation can render wonderful help in teaching Social Studies. Many teachers feel that they cannot properly write on black board. But let it be mentioned here that this skill is necessary for every teacher whether he teaches Social Studies, or Language, Maths Science or any other subject. It is true that for teaching Social Studies many types of maps, charts, graphs, outlines are available in the market. But it cannot be denied that the best ones are those which are prepared in the presence of pupils. The chart of the map that is drawn in the presence of the pupils is formable beneficial than the one already drawn before hand. That is why ability to draw a sketch or a good picture on the black board by the teacher is so much important. Do not crowd the aids at anyone time. To emphasise different points, ideas and concepts pieces of chalk of different colours be used and the work to be done should be planned in advance.

Importance of Black-Board/Chalk-Board

If it is used properly it become highly inspirational. It helps the pupils a lot to grasp the write-up. While teaching a lesson, any picture displayed, can draw the attention of the class. By writing on the black-board of drawing sketches, the teacher can emphasise the main points. Using lines, he can draw and present to the class, a map or a picture. Black-board is a means which is ever present in the class. For its use neither technical knowledge nor the skill of high artistic nature is required.

Use of Black-Board/Chalk-Board

In teaching of Social Studies the use of the black-board/chalk-board can be made as follows:

1. To write summary
2. To explain the relationship and importance of a name or a term

3. To write outlines of a plan
4. To present chart, line drawing, graph or symbolic representation
5. To explain the sequence of a thing
6. To give main instruction
7. To write rules and definition
8. To give information relating to dates, table, statistics etc.

IMPORTANT FACTS RELATING TO THE USE OF BLACK-BOARD

The Social Studies teacher, while using the black-board, should keep the following in mind:

1. Before starting the class-work collect all necessary things; duster, chalk, scale, stencils, protector etc.
2. Rub off the Black-Board with the duster, and not by fingers.
3. Start writing on it from the left hand top corner. Write only important points on it. Remember that it is not suitable for extensive work.
4. Plan in advance what to write on it. Do not draw/display any map before hand or take help of any book continuously.
5. Use a pointer to focus attention of the pupils on the map or drawing sketched on it.
6. It should be located at a place so as to be visible to all pupils with facility. Let there be no reflection of light on it. It should not be at a greater height of the vision level of the pupils, and the desks in the front row should be at least eight feet away from the black board.
7. Write neatly and uniformly on it. In addition whatever may be written on it, should be in a serial order, so that pupils develop habit to write in a sequence.
8. The letters written on it, should be bold so that pupils may easily see them. Words in small size should not be

written on it. What ever be written on it, should be in straight lines.

9. While writing on it, teacher should not cover it, but standing at the angle of 45°, he should write on it. If he does not do that, chances of indiscipline will arise in the class.
10. While writing on it, at times, the teacher should cast a glance at pupils.
11. It should be repainted at least once a year.
12. After writing on it, he should stand on one side of the black-board. He should surprise the class and attend to individual difficulties of pupils. He should do this so that each pupil can see every-thing written on it.
13. As he writes on it, he should speak out the same simultaneously.

The conclusion is that the black-board/chalk-board is an important aid in teaching this subject.

VISUAL AIDS

1. Real Objects. If during teaching, real objects are used as teaching aids, their impact will be far greater than that of all other types of aids. If the parts of the plots are to be taught, then the lesson may be taught with the help of the real plant. This will create in pupil a sense of joy and interest. So, as far as possible, real objects alone be used as teaching aids, like bones, feathers of the bird, specimens of claws, butterflies, leaves, flower, metalic coins, specimens of rocks, machine and tools, tickets etc. To stock them is the best course. Specimen of different types of corn can be stored in small bottles. Put the flower or leaf on the blotting paper and press the same tinder a heavy book and in four to five days, it will take flat shape. Preserve it in a file. Fine and scarce objects may be displayed, putting them in glass containers or almirahs. For example, take the coins of the period of Samudra Gupta. On one side of the coin is depicted Samudra Gupta playing on a voilin. This gives the knowledge of his love for music and his adeptness, in playing on the voilin. In the same way, take up the fifty-paisa coin of the present period of Indian government. On it is displayed the image of Pt. Jawaharlal Nehru. In its bottom is inscribed 1889-1964 which tells about the birth and death years of his life. On the backside of the coin the national symbol is there and the denomination of the coin and 'Bharat' is indicated in English and Hindi languages. This coin easily gives us knowledge about the economic condition of India. State language and about the birth and demise of Pt. Nehru. Hence coins are powerful aids in explaining the past.

2. Map. These have a special importance in teaching of Social Studies/Science since maps are mostly, used in teaching of history and geography. Readymade maps are available in the market, but if the teacher shows to pupils by himself drawing the maps, it effect will be altogether different. The maps should show names and other necessary symbols. Maps should be clear and neatly drawn. Geographical situations and knowledge of distance, areas, actual location of various regions can be given to pupils—with the help of maps. Maps can be relating, to economics, political science, civics, social studies, history and geography etc. Let teachers put more emphasis on their use, in the schools. The pupils will acquire real knowledge thereby. Maps are drawn also in the atlas. These can be made of paper, cloth iron walls. The pre-historic man used to draw maps on the bark of the tree or on the stones. To study geography, it is necessary to know the earth in the form of a big family so that he can understand what families of the world live at what places and what things are found in abundance and where those are scarce. Also it tells us which parts of the world lag behind and which are more progressive. The whole universe in real form, cannot be presented in the class, nor can the activities of the world can be shown otherwise. Map is the only aid through which the world can be presented in the class.

Free Hand Drawing of Map

It helps in copying down the printed maps on the black board. The map should be clear and fine. In it, the directions, mountains, oceans, industries should be clearly shown. It should be hung at a place so that all pupils can see it. The teacher should put questions and pupils be encouraged to show the indicated spots. The teacher should encourage pupils to fill up maps, so that the pupils remain active and their interest is sustained and get permanent knowledge. In the lower classes practice should be given to fill-in maps with coloured pencils so that no difficulty is faced in higher classes. The map should be used only when the occasion arises and later on it may be removed, otherwise it will continue to engage the attention of the pupils. Thus, with the use of maps the teacher can give correct knowledge to pupils about districts, countries, foreign land and the geographical situation of the world.

Uses of Maps

The teacher should cultivate in pupils; interest for acquiring complete information from the maps. In the first instance he should ask them to prepare a map of the classroom then of their homes and later on from home to school, distance and next, pupils may be asked to draw the map of their state. When interest and knowledge develops then they can prepare maps with imagination.

1. Maps show the routes *e.g.* roads, canals, dams, welfare centres, social education centres, adult education centres, high schools etc. where they exist.
2. Maps help in giving the knowledge of distance *e.g.*, at what distances are Delhi, Kolkata, Sikanderabad, Chandigarh, Faridabad etc. from your city.
3. With topographical maps, correct ideas can be had about altitude, rivers, valleys, mountains etc. of any place.
4. Maps give information relating to cultural, physical and geographical features of a place. For example, altitude from sea level, thickly populated countries, thinly populated countries and developed countries etc.
5. Maps help in making a comparative study of rainfall, climate, pressure, seasons and climatic changes at different places.
6. Maps give knowledge about climate *i.e.* where it is too hot and where it is too cold.

7. With symbolic language, maps can show, rail routes, roads, cities, oceans, plateau, valleys, level ground etc. Idea can easily be formed of the distance.
8. Maps can help in making comparison between two countries, regions and cities.
9. Maps give knowledge about the directions *e.g.* North, South, East and West. In the map of India, historical, industrial, places worth visiting, small figures of the same can be pasted. They can draw a map of the building of the school, showing class location and roads leading from the school to different parts of the city.
10. Maps can give information relating to countries, regions and of the world regarding different productions, population, and minerals.

3. Diagrams. To explain an object, fully, a diagram is drawn with the lines. To give clear and proper knowledge in science and geography teachers use diagrams. In drawing diagrams no expenditure is incurred and no special duration of time is required.

1. Diagram drawn on the black board then and there has a lasting impact on the children.
2. To explain, plants and flowers in Botany and display of different parts of human body, in life science, the diagrams can be drawn on the black-board.
3. While showing the diagrams, real objects or film strips and pictures can also be shown. That will have more lasting impact. Diagrams should be simple so that those can be easily understood. Diagrams should be suitable to the topic. In order to explain the meaning, the teacher may use coloured pieces of chalk, from time to time to make diagrams attractive.

All topics of the syllabus and all kinds of subject-matter, can be expressed with the help of diagrams as visual aids. But the success of this depends upon the fact that the diagrams and symbols be made the medium of expression which can be fully grasped by the pupils and the meaning of which they can understand properly. For example, the diagrams displaying the internal structure of the power, of the ear or of the eye along with the functioning cannot be properly explained unless the pupils thoroughly know in advance the symbols used in the diagrams. Hence the diagrams do not render any help in so far as the teaching of the subject-matter in the initial stage is concerned. In subsequent stage, that is of presentation or of study or of recapitulation, the diagrams can play an important role.

4. Chart. It is visual aid through which pupils can be acquainted with clear pictures of the subject-matter. The use of charts, enhances learning process. The use of charts can be done easily and effectivity in all subjects. They are available readmade in the market. If these are not available in the market, then the teacher himself can prepare them suitable to the lesson. The figures in the charts must be big enough so that the pupils sitting in all corners can be benefited. Small figures kill the interest of the pupil and they have to face inconvenience. There is a fear of indiscipline in the class. The picture drawn on the chart must be clear and definite.

Charts are of various types. The teacher may get charts prepared relevant to the topic and can use the same as a teaching devices. Some of them are as under:

(i) ***Time Chart.*** It can be called the time table. These are presented mostly, in accordance with historical/chronological events, period, different rulers and battles. These show the time span of events and develop time sense.

(ii) ***Table Chart.*** In these charts heads are drawn under which events/accounts are given. These give the serial order of historical events, of rulers, of wars and the list of the same, according to time.

(iii) ***Picture Chart.*** Various pictures are collected and shown in the chart *i.e.*, means of transport, means of irrigation, postal agencies etc.

(iv) ***Tree Chart.*** It can show the gradual development of a thing. The trunk of the tree is the main form and the branches show the development. Best examples are in botany, regarding the development of plants of insects in zoology. Just as branches and leaves sprout from the trunk, the chart develops in the same way.

(v) ***Flow Chart.*** In these charts the sequential growth of an object can be shown or the rise and fall of the monarchs can also be shown. Charts can also be made of the structure and development of law.

(vi) ***Graphical Chart.*** These are used to show statistical figures as of population growth, rise and fall in prices, trade, rainfall etc.

(vii) ***Pictorial Chart.*** That which displays small picture *e.g.*, rice bag, wheat sacks, animal pictures.

(viii) ***Graph Chart.*** Such charts are used in teaching geography and Social Studies, these are used to display statistical figures *e.g.*, rainfall and temperature, rainfall and population growth etc. These are of five kinds—area, picture, line, length, graph etc.

5. Posters. Posters have special importance in teaching of Social Studies/Science. In a way, posters are the pictures of things, persons, places and events but in them the pictorial expression, as of the pictures, is not quite clear and in a direct way but with a special angle and indirect and symbolic form. General pictures can present entire description of the subject-matter. Through poster, one idea is made the point of focus and a forceful emotional appeal is made, whichever special message or a particular fact is supposed to inspire the pupils, and it fully captures their mind and heart that is why, in the world of advertisement and publicity its help is taken to the extent of which no other material is put through posters. Due to their different style these create an imposing environment so as to change or modify a trend or to inspire an action by which the role is played not only for bringing about desirable modifications in the behaviour of the individual only but also to turn the masses in the desired direction and full help can be got in propagating specific plans and movements.

To convey a message to pupils in an attractive manner, instruction given through posters is considered to be good. Posters can be on any subject, so as to cast influence on the pupils. Attractive posters have few words. The picture, cartoon or a diagram are presented in a fine way, so that pupils catch the message quickly. The thought in the posters should be clear and the same should be set in a chain so that the feeling could be caught. The choice of colours and contrasts should be appropriate. The writing on the poster should be big in size so that pupils can see the same vividly. With the help of these posters, the teacher leaves a lasting impact on the children, about teeth, ear, eyes, washing of clothes, harm done by eating polluted stuff, importance of cleanliness etc. Posters can be prepared with the help of cuttings and clippings, magazine, pictures etc. Posters are prepared on paper, wood, cloth and plywood in different colours. They can be of any size. So, the sources for getting posters by the teacher are put under two groups, the external and internal. Outside the school whatever can be obtained from the advertising and publicity agencies of the community, and suitable selection can be made out of the same. The teacher with the help of the pupils, and under his personal influence, should try to stock them. In the form of personal source also, the school, using the creative talents of the pupils, should try to prepare posters. In their preparation, collection and use, the following things should be borne in mind.

(i) The educational utility of the posters must be given more importance and only those posters should be collected or prepared which can help achieve specific instructional objectives.

(ii) The class teacher should use only those posters which help the pupils to understand properly, and which can play forceful role in bringing about expected modification in their behaviour.

(iii) The class teacher should select and use posters keeping in mind the proportion relating to clarity, simplification, attractive force, and to focus thoughts and stir emotion.

BULLETIN BOARD

For both the teacher and the student the bulletin board is a sheet of wood, masonite, cork, celetex, or similar material set within a frame. Used for displaying pictures, charts, posters, clippings, photographs, or other learning materials, it serves as a perpetual magazine for the students of social studies. It gives information of direct concern to the pupils and tap their curiosity and desire for knowledge. It provides a practical outlet for artistic talent and creative ability. It helps to unify class spirit by creating a sense of responsibility, appreciation an accomplishment. It stimulates student's interest and enthusiasm for, a particular lesson. The bulletin board must be simple. It should telegraph its message quickly, easily and efficiently. The materials must be changed frequently. Tendency to overload the bulletin board must be resisted. Display must be done neatly and well.

Possibilities of Use

Unlimited possibilities of use exist for effective bulletin board displays. These might depict any number of themes such as agriculture through the ages, media of communication, political parties in the country, elections, food, fads and fallacies, etc. These use such materials as cartoons, newspapers, book jackets, ribbons or coloured strings, posters, snap shots, etc. Displays can be developed to illustrate local history, industrial achievements, famous personalities, foreign lands and people, various products, etc. Maps, drawings, graphs and pictures may be combined to present facts, stir the imagination and call for action on anyone of these themes.

Displays on the bulletin board should be attractive, appropriate, meaningful, timely and interesting. These may include pictures, posters pamphlets, cartoons, graphs, maps, charts, diagrams, news-items, feature articles, magazine articles and samples of pupil's creative work. A judicious selection of such displays should be made after critical inspection and approval by teacher or the committee appointed for this purpose. Each display should be a unit, containing one central theme.

Suggestions to use the Bulletin Board Effectively

1. Display interesting and understandable material on the bulletin board.
2. Rebate the material should, to the topics being studied in the class.
3. Change the material according to purposes and problems.
4. Make balanced and artistic arrangements with appropriate headings, titles, explanatory notes, mountings and colours etc., to make the display meaningful.
5. Give ample opportunities to the pupils to explore to and discuss the material displayed or to be displayed on the bulletin board.
6. Give the pupils opportunities to assist in arranging and re-arranging materials, which they have prepared or brought from home, for display.

Flannel Board

The flannel board is somewhat like a blackboard. But it has added advantages of colour, movement and quick removal, leading to more interest and more learning. Its extreme flexibility permits various arrangements to be tried experimentally. Though flannel boards are not used as extensively in Social Studies as in other subjects, it is a very useful teaching aid which must be tried and used effectively by Social Studies teachers. "It is especially helpful in presenting events or ideas in sequence as a story unfolds, a report is given, demonstration is performed, steps in process are given or basic concepts are presented in a definite order."

Suggestions to use a Flannel Board in Social Studies

1. Cut sections of a large map and show on the flannel board in sequence as the new territory was added while teaching

a unit or territorial expansion. Expansion of Marhatta rule, or British rule in India can very profitably be explained with the help of flannel board.

2. Prepare charts showing different agencies of a city or state or union government and use on the flannel board to explain the structure of these governments.

3. Prepare coloured time-lines in sections for any period or movement and show with advantage on the flannel board.

MAPS IN SOCIAL STUDIES

In history and geography all agree that maps play an important role in teaching. The chief purpose in using maps in history is to fix place relationship in pupil's mind. They help the students to visualise important place mentioned in the text-books, of history. In geography, they show definite facts of position, relief, climate, vegetation, minerals, population, crops and industries.

Sketch Maps. The teacher of Social Studies should supplement the use of wall maps by drawing sketch maps on the blackboard they are drawn to give prominence to, a few places, points, regions, relief features, etc. Students also show interest in that topic because they also copy it on their note-books. The students should purchase outline exercise books and should fill in the maps.

Globe. Map is flat but it represents a round surface on a flat surface. The student cannot comprehend the relationships and locations of the different countries continents and direction. To give a correct view of all these, frequent use of the globe should be made. It has its value in showing the relationship of continents and oceans. The day and night formation, the phenomena of seasons, the longitude and latitude, ocean and air routes, etc. No device can be more helpful in expanding one's concept of the earth than the globe.

Atlas. Every student of Social Studies must purchase an atlas. They should make use of the atlas in and outside the classroom. They should themselves locate the physical features, rivers, industries on the map whenever they are studying text-books of geography and history or newspapers.

Printed maps, outline sketch maps and atlases have their own place. As a useful and necessary and are complimentary to one another.

Charts and Diagrams

A diagram is a useful device of recording what you know with brevity and charity. Ready-made diagrams and charts are available in the market. Some of them, no doubt, are useful summaries of important facts including excellent photographs etc. yet the students should be encouraged to prepare their own charts and diagrams as these are more educative, economical and easier to understand. Facts depicted in the diagram remain more vividly and clearly in the minds of the pupils and it facilitates memorising and revision of facts of Social Studies.

Non-Verbal Child

The non-verbal child, who is poor in language, feels satisfies when he gives outlet to his thought through diagrams. Diagrams in geography, history, economics save him from disappointment.

A Few Hints for Drawing Diagrams

The following points should be borne in mind while preparing diagrams:

1. A good diagram should present facts in a simple and accurate manner. There should be no over-crowding of facts.
2. Visual aids as photos or pictures should be fixed on a chart to increase their visual appeal.
3. In lettering, size of the word is propedy adjusted to the size of the paper.
4. Colours should be used for classification, contrast and comparison.

Time Charts. Development of time sense in history is a very important aim. Time sense implies three relationship—distance, duration and location. Which means that a student must know how long ago a particular incident of history took place, and for how long did it continue and what is its relation to other incidents in history. To explain these time relations, we have to rely on dates. Time charts are of two forms—*(i)* Time line and *(ii)* Time graphs.

(i) Time Lines. Certain historical dates are to be presented to students simultaneously. A teacher may draw a line, say 10 centimetres representing a century. Dates should be plotted on the left and events on the right side of it. The relative distances will show the location, duration and distance of various events in history.

(ii) Time Graphs. Graphs are made useful to show the development of political, economic or social movements in history. Along the X-axis we plot the tariff or the years and along the Y-axis we plot the events showing size and fall of a particular king or dynasty. For example, we can plot the size and fall of Mughal power showing size of mughal power from 1526 reaching its climax in the period of Aurangzeb and then declining till the time of Indian War of Independence in 1857, when it totally collapsed.

Comparative graphs are very important to show relative developments. We can make comparative graphs from Indian and British history and can, thus show the stage of culture and civilization in the two countries.

MODELS AND SPECIMEN

Original material objects and sources may not be approachable due to a variety of difficulties. Models can be easily used as a substitute of original thing. In history, we may make models of great rulers and important personalities, armours and weapons, forts, pillars and rock inscriptions, a model of the First Battle of Panipat, model of the earth or various dams. Models may be made out of clay, plaster of paris, plasticine, paper pulp etc.

The specimen has the enormous advantages of being not a picture, a reproduction, or a model, but the reality specimen of crops, rocks, minerals, textile goods can be shown to the students.

BlackBoard. A blackboard is never failing frend of a teacher. The blackboard although not in itself a visual aid can be so used and the possibilities of its use are beyond limit. The effectiveness of use of blackboard depends upon the skill of a teacher. The following are the uses of the black-board.

1. To make summary of the contents
2. To develop an outline
3. To draw a sketch map, diagram
4. To draw dateline-timeline

TABLES

In social studies we are concerned with statistics about the various political, social and economic developments for which data has to be analysed. Tables are used for presenting data in a convenient and visual form. These tables make data intelligible and comprehensible. For example, the growth in production, industrial output, imports, exports, literacy, development, etc., can be easily shown in the table form.

The pupils should be made aware of the fact that the figures given in the tables are not for learning by heart but for the quantitative ideal they suggest and political, social and economic perspective they create.

Suggestions for using Tables

1. ***Intelligibility.*** Make the tables intelligible, meeting the requirements of the pupils at a particular age-group.
2. ***Posting Data.*** Post the data in the tables in a neat manner.
3. ***Economise the Time of Learning.*** Impart maximum knowledge in the shortest possible time.

Following figure shows population by religion in India in table form.

POPULATION BY RELIGION IN INDIA

TABLE

Religious group	1961 Number (million)	1961 Percent to total	1971 Number (million)	1971 Percent to total	1981 Number (million)	1981 Percent to total	1991 Number (million)	1991 Percent to total
Hindus	366.5	83.5	453.4	82.7	549.7	82.6	672.6	82.41
Muslims	46.9	10.7	61.4	11.2	75.6	11.4	95.2	11.67
Christians	10.7	2.4	14.3	2.6	16.2	2.4	18.9	2.32
Sikhs	7.8	1.8	10.4	1.9	13.1	2.0	16.3	1.99
Buddhists	3.2	0.7	3.9	0.7	4.7	0.7	6.3	0.77
Jains	2.0	0.5	2.6	0.5	3.2	0.5	3.4	0.41
Other	1.6	0.4	2.2	0.4	2.8	0.4	3.5	0.43
Total	439.2	100.0	548.2	100.0	665.3	100.0	816.2	100.00

GRAPHS

Graphs are flat pictures employing dots, lines or pictures to visualise numerical and statistical data to show statistics or relationships. Made according to exact specifications they depict specifically quantitative data for analysis, interpretation or comparison. Uses Graphs are effective tools for making comparison and contrast. The use of visual imageries for abstract ideas in graphs helps clarification and remembrance.

Kinds of Graphs

1. ***Line Graph.*** It is used when there are a considerable number of continuous data to be plotted. The concepts are represented with the help of vertically or horizontally drawn simple line. Variations of the line graph include the high, low and shaded line graph. Pictorial illustrations and cartoons are used on line graphs to increase their interest and readability. As it provides more contrast. A shaded line graph attracts more than a solid line graph.

2. ***Bar Graph.*** It consists of bars arranged horizontally or vertically from a 'Zero' base. Size, length and colour of the

bars represent different values. The bar graph is best employed when the number of values to be compared is small not more than five or six. These are helpful in comparing or contrasting many subjects such as comparisons of income and wages, quotas, sales, etc. The data in the bar graph are summarized vividly in the pictorical element at the right of the graph.

3. ***Pictorial Graph.*** It is an outstanding method of graphic representation. In it pictures are used for the expression of ideas. These are more attractive and easily understood. In them a complete story is told with pictures. The number or size of the pictures conveys the proportionate amount. Pictorial graph is not as exact as other types of graph because there is a certain amount of estimation on quantity.

4. ***Circle Graph.*** It is a circle, the sections of which are used to represent component parts of a whole. Such information can be typically represented on circle graphs as the distribution of expenditures of a municipality, distribution of money on different subjects in the five-year plans, distribution of money on different types of education.

   Two characteristics are common to all circle graphs. 1. They always present totals or whole amounts and, 2. Their parts or segments are calculated in percentages or fractional parts of a whole.

5. ***The Flannel Graph.*** It is a dynamic instructional tool making teaching and learning of social studies real, lasting and entertaining. It helps the teacher to present vivid and meaningful associated pictures or symbols to the class. The graphic cutouts can be used by the teacher like ready coins. They do not need thumb tacks, chalk, light switches to turn-off and on, darkened rooms, unfamiliar machines or equipment to deal with. The flannel material sticks to the flannel board lending magic and colour. Because of the simplicity of its construction, its utility and adaptability in

instruction it is used by teachers of social studies as a very useful tool of teaching.

Uses of Graphs

Being symbolic and abstract in character graphs are best used in the body and summary of a lesson after the student has acquired a background of information from other sources. Graph is best used as a summarizing device.

MAPS

Maps are flat representations of the earth's surface which convey information by means of lines, symbols, words and colours. These are essential for the teaching of social studies. A teacher of the social studies is directly concerned with two most important abstracts place and time. Every happening occurs in a definite place and in a fixed time. Maps are the universally accepted symbols for the representation of space. As a record of spatial concepts the map tells a story as nothing else can do. As place of the happening has some influence over the course of the happening, therefore, proper use of the map helps a lot.

Making of Maps. Maps on flat sheets of paper are far easier to carry about and to store. On such flat sheets of paper the social studies teacher can show distances and bearings for countries of reasonable size climate, the races of man, the types of rock and minerals, the comparative size of towns, etc. Today's techniques of colour printing enable us to show the earth's mountains, river valleys and plateaus in striking relief.

Uses of Maps

A map is a very useful tool for the geographer the motorists, the scout, the guide, the civil defence personnel, the administrator and the armed forces. Rudyard Kipling rightly says, "Intelligent participation in any discussion requires a knowledge of a map of the world."

Map Work by the Pupils

As maps are a combination of lines, symbols, colours and terms, pupils should be able to 'read' the maps. Maps are the most valuable historical documents. An Indian student of history may learn the unexpected trouble on the northern borders and our comparative ignorance about the terrain and inhospitable climate there is called 'map literacy'. Children should be taught the art of map reading. They should be able to interpret and re-translate the symbols and lines on the map into hills and valleys, rivers and fields, etc., map involves six comprehensive skills.

(i) Orienting the map and noting directions

(ii) Recognising the scale of a map and computing distances

(iii) Reading map symbols

(iv) Expressing relative locations

(v) Locating places on maps and globes by means of good systems

(vi) Comparing maps and making inferences.

Types of Maps

1. ***Relief Maps.*** These are models of the geographical features of a place. They are used where geographical features have a direct influence on the course of events. For example, relief map of India can be very useful to show terrains all over the country.

2. ***Flat Maps.*** Flat maps are of different kinds, for example, political, physical, population, economic, rainfall, temperature, soil and vegetation, roads and the like are very useful. Flat maps may be used for showing campaigns, treaties, boundaries, routes of armies, routes of travels, etc.

3. ***Sketch Maps.*** These are maps in outline which are used according to necessity. These maps are useful in showing the course of action followed by an invader, *e.g.*, Mohammad Gauri, Mahmud Gaznavi.

Use of Maps

1. ***Outline.*** A simple outline map should be used in the class for the purpose of teaching. The relevant points may be

developed in the map in course of teaching. For example, the map to show the extension of the empire under Akbar should start with an outline map of India, showing the places under the control of Akbar at the time of his accession. New places may be indicated on the map as his conquests are presented to the pupils, one after the other. The individual pupils should also possess outline maps to fill them as the lesson progresses and the map presented to the class is developed as a whole.

2. ***Flannelographs.*** In lower classes use of flannelographs, an outline of map may be fixed on the flannelograph and the relevant places or objects—forts, battlefields, capitals, routes of invasions, travels, etc., may be placed inside the boundry of the map in appropriate places as the lesson advances. Use of flannelographs gives dramatic effect to the use of maps. It provides opportunities for activities to pupils.
3. ***Use of Electric Devices.*** These can used for making the presentation of maps interesting. The place to which attention is to be drawn, may be illuminated by the pressing of buttons which proves effective in the primary and junior secondary classes.
4. ***Interesting.*** Maps should be able to arouse students' interest.
5. ***Accurate.*** Maps should be accurate and up-to-date.
6. ***Pupils Map.*** While the maps are presented to the class, the pupils should work on their own maps. This will sustain their interest. While pupils in the middle and secondary classes could draw maps themselves. Children in the primary classes may be given printed outlines for filling in details.
7. ***Understanding Symbols.*** Conventional symbols used for land, water, elevation, railways, roads, etc., must be taught to the pupils so that they may understand the symbolism of the map. The pupils must also be able to see beyond them. They must remember that dot represents Delhi, the wavy

line represents Brahmaputra or the brown patch represents the Deccan Plateau.

8. ***Timing.*** Maps should be used at the appropriate time. Like an experiment in science, map is an integral part of the work in a subject. It is not something to be taught apart from the subject.

MODELS

Model may be termed as a recognisable three-dimensional representation of a real thing. It reduces large objects to a size convenient for observation. It produces interior view of objects normally covered or otherwise invisible. In it non-essentials are removed so that fundamentals can be more readily observed.

Models are suitable substitutes for most of the historical remains and geographical phenomena giving a vivid impression of the real. They may be managed to the class with greater facility than large objects. A river valley electric project for example, may be so large and so complicated as to be difficult to observe even when on the ground, while a good model may bring the whole scene within a single sweep of the eye with all its essentials.

Traits of Good Model

1. ***Accurate.*** A good model must be accurate. Crude representation model has no place in the teaching of social studies, which required truthful representation. The purpose of historical or geographical model is to impress pupil's blind through the medium of the eye. It should not expose them to inaccuracy in imparting essentials.
2. ***Simple.*** A good model should not be obscured or complicated. It should have the necessary simplicity.
3. ***Light and Handy.*** A good model should be light and handy. These traits lead to its effectiveness.
4. ***Useful.*** A good model must be able to help in the illustration of some dermite facts.

5. ***Ingenuine.*** A good model is an expression of the innate capacity and potentiality of the student.
6. ***Solid.*** A good model in order to be effective must be solidity *i.e.* solidity in its inherent strength to resist.

Models used in Teaching of Social Studies

1. *Models of Personalities.* These refer to those who have made specific contributions in specific fields such as political, religious, social, economic and cultural. These help pupils to identify themselves with these personalities, thus making more meaningful and interesting making every event connected with them. Such models are particularly useful in the junior classes.

2. *Models of Armours and Weapons of Different Ages.* These can be particularly used for class dramatisations and exhibitions.

3. *Models of Pillars and Rock Inscriptions.* These add to the effectiveness of social studies lessons.

4. *Models of Places.* These models refer to sites of events of the great historical importance, for example, Kurukshetra, Panipat, and Plassey, etc. used in exhibitions they may develop the pupil's interest in the study of history.

5. *Models of Human Dwellings.* Utensils, ornaments, costumes, etc., in different ages besides ordinary social studies lessons. These are also used for class dramatisations and exhibitions.

6. *Models Illustrating Agriculture, Means of Transport and Communication, etc.,* through the Ages. These create interest in the process of development. These impress upon the students how man progressed from stage to stage.

7. *Models of Architecture and Sculpture.* Available from commercial films these are useful in developing proper concepts.

8. *Models of Documents or Copper Plates.* These help in teaching social studies by the source method.

9. *Models of Gods and Goddesses.* These refer to those worshipped during the different ages. These help in creating proper awareness among pupils about the process of religious development.

10. ***Visuals Depicting Life in the Different Regions of the World.*** These are useful for conveying information on how people live in the different parts of the world.

11. ***Models of Dams and Projects.*** These may be about more famous dams and projects.

12. ***Models in Relief.*** These may be about different countries.

13. ***Models of Distribution of Minerals.*** These may be about different countries.

Though models may be purchased whenever necessary but it is better if there are prepared through the joint efforts of teachers and pupils. A great variety of materials is used in model preparation, such as cardboard, paper, papier-mache clay, wood, bamboo, plaster of paris, plasticine, metals, plastics, strings etc.

GLOBE

The globe is the most accurate representation of the earth available in the classroom. Simple and inexhaustible source to help the students it is a combination of a model and a map. It is a map with a curved surface. Therefore, it is a more accurate than the model with a flat surface. It simplifies the mysteries of the world. It is best in expanding one's conception of the earth. It provides a correct concept of the Arctic and Antarctic circles, the Axis of the earth, hemispheres, latitudes longitudes, meridian, prime-meridian and the poles, seasons, rotations and revolutions of the earth location and relationship of different parts of the world and land and sea routes etc.

Use of Globe

1. In Social Studies pupils should be taught to get correct information from the globe. They should be able to locate countries, mountains and rivers etc. For the comparison and contrast of different areas of the world pupils should be taught how to read and interpret the globe.
2. The globe should be used to develop fundamental concepts about the earth and its surface features.

3. The globe may be used in primary to develop concepts of the roundness of the earth, directions, how three-fourths of earth's surface is covered by water, how surface features differ from place to place and how major land areas and water bodies differ in size.
4. In secondary classes the globe may be used to develop concepts of the formation of day and night, changes in seasons, rotation and revolution of the earth and latitudes and longitudes of this kind. Concept development essential to the development of map-reading and map drawing skills, so useful for understanding major geographic concepts.

MECHANICAL AIDS

1. Radio. The importance of radio in this age of educational technology is not hidden from any body. It is considered to be an effective audio-aid the educational lessons broadcast by the A.I.R. greatly benefit students scattered far and wide. Radio Station broadcast lectures of education and of other scholars the benefit of which is reaped by all pupils A list is released in advance of the lessons to be broadcast by the A.I.R. So, the head of the school or the concerned teachers should have knowledge in advance of such educational programmes. One more advantage of educational broadcast is that one can listen to special talk or the composition of an artist, again and again, by tape recording it. The radio discussion on election, civic duties, rights, problems of the country and other allied fixture is of great importance in teaching Social Studies. Radio broadcast is of two types:

(i) ***Ordinary Broadcast.*** Under it general information is given relating to general events and circumstances.

(ii) ***Educational Broadcast.*** These are specially prepared for pupils. These are broadcast as radio lessons with a view to achieve definite educational objectives.

Use of Radio in Teaching of Social Studies/Sciences

(a) In the first instance, the teacher should study available literature relating to lessons. It includes a list of programmes and the time-table of daily broadcast.

(b) On the basis of the collected information and linking it with the subject, he should prepare a plan for pupils to listen to the lesson broadcast carefully.

(c) For radio relay, attention should be paid to the geographical, conditions. Proper arrangement regarding seats, the receiver set, light and air, should be made. There should be no noise in the classroom while the relay is on.

(d) The teacher should motivate pupils so that they are mentally prepared to listen to the radio broadcast with attention and interest. The teacher should set the radio in the subject room concerned and the entire class need not be taken to that room.

(e) After the broadcast, there should be follow-up and there should be a discussion on the lesson relayed. Pupils should get time for getting their doubts removed. The teacher should ask pupils to take down notes while the relay is on. After the relay is over, time may be allowed to pupils to remove their difficulties which may have been there in their notes. If in the course of the relay, a pupil puts a question, he should not be allowed to do so. He may be instructed in advance to note in the exercise book, a question that he wants to put and he should put it after the broadcast ends.

Utility of Radio in Social Studies Teaching

- It offers opportunities to listen to the thoughts of eminent scientists, educators, linguists and about art, which is not possible, otherwise for every person or pupil, individually.
- It is of a great importance for areas flung far and wide.
- Being less expensive, every body can make rise of it.
- It greatly helps the teacher in achieving educational goals.
- With population growth, the instructional facilities offered by radio lessons are increasing daily.
- The teacher himself gets knowledge from the radio broadcasts because these are prepared by experts. He comes to know several newfacts, principles etc.

2. Tape Recorder. With this instrument, voice is recorded. It has three parts-microphone, amplifier and reproducer.

There are two main activities in this instrument: one to record the voice and second to reproduce it. It is easy to play a tape recorder. All the buttons of the tape recorder, clearly mention that to start, it is written 'Play' and to stop it 'Stop' and the word 'Record' is written for recording any speech or song.

Tape recorder should be place on a level surface. The recorded stuff from it can also be erased and in its place again a new matter can be recorded.

Tape recorder can be of great use in music, language, dramatics. It can remove defects in speaking and can reform pronunciation. Tape recorder helps a good deal in re-inforcement and evaluation in micro-teaching. It helps in preparing commentaries on film slides. It helps the teacher also in bringing modification in his behaviour. Having recorded the educationally important talks and other programmes, it can be fully re-listened at any time.

Tape recorder has a great utility in the teaching of Social Studies Science. Whenever seminars are organised on a subject, the tape recorder is set to record it. So, from time to time the same can be available for listening in the class and pupils can be motivated on the subject and a discussion can be arranged.

3. Teaching Machine. It plays a prominent part in teaching process for the pupils of Social Studies/Science. Teaching machine is mechanical electrical device. This presents a brief programme at a time. A pupil handles this machine. It reads aloud, whatever stuff is put in it and has to answer it itself. Immediate correct answer coming forth for re-inforcement.

In the words of Edward B. Fry, "Teaching machines are defined as automatic, partially automatic, devices which present a question or other stimulus to provide a means of response, and then informs him of the correctness of his response immediately after he has responded."

In Social Studies/Science teaching the basic utilities of teaching machine, are as under:

1. These devices teach the pupils without the teacher.
2. They make pupils active.
3. Pupils move according to respective speed. Every pupil has to answer questions put in the programmed matter.
4. In some teaching machines, facility is available for presenting outline for group instruction.
5. Some teaching machines, demand answer to multiple choice questions.
6. The teaching machine is operated with hands or by power.
7. When the pupil responds, the teaching machine gives him the correct answer so that he may go ahead.
8. Its purpose is for individual instruction.

4. Projector. Projector or Magic Lantern is considered to be one of the most ancient inventions in projecting aids. It is also known as diascope or slide projector. Projector helps in enlarging the figures in the slide.

In this the slide is invertly inserted and by casting strong light rays, through the medium of glass, its magnified form is projected on the screen.

In the teaching of Social science, it occupies a special place. With the help of projector we can show spread of diseases, the size/shape of the mosquito, diseases caused by dirty water, the reproductive functioning of the mosquitoes etc. which are too subtle, but are magnified by the projector, on the screen. In this way, the teacher becomes efficient in making teaching of Social Studies, interesting.

Utility of the Projector in Teaching of Social Studies/Sciences

1. Before showing the slide to the pupils, if the teacher gives them some information regarding the topic it will have more psychological impact on them.

2. It is a convenient aid, and can be used in the class at any time and place.
3. The teacher should continue throwing hints and explain while the slide is being shown.

5. Epidiascope. As the name goes, this aid is made of two constituents—episcope and diascope *i.e.* it represents the combined form of the magic lantern. For this it is not necessary to prepare a slide. Any opaque thing can be straight way shown on the screen, the diagram of which is given in the book and is difficult to draw. It takes time to sketch it on the blackboard. Moreover, the figure on the blackboard is not drawn well. So, in teaching of Social Studies/ Science, the projection of these figures, with the help of epidiascope, can be shown to pupil, on the screen.

It is of special utility for pupils. If in the class, there is a pupil with good hand or has prepared a good picture, then with the help of epidiascope it can be show to pupils, on the screen to motivate them.

6. Films. Films are also effective teaching aids. These also affect all senses of the pupils. To show them in the class the teacher should know in advance about the subject. Before showing to the pupils; the teacher should see it himself so that with, his teaching he may be able to coordinate the subject-matter of the film Before showing the film to the pupils they must be mentally prepared so that they may be motivated fully tó see it. Before showing the film, arrangement should be made properly for pupils sitting, air, light etc. The projector must also be tested before hand. The pupils must be encouraged for exchange of views. The teacher and pupils should simultaneously take down notes. For more clarity, some part of the film may be shown again. It is necessary to have an evaluation of the impact of the film on pupils. They should be offered opportunities to express their ideas freely. They should be given opportunities to use the information in a practical way.

Since the films have proved useful in exercising psychological influence on pupils, their utility is great in the teaching of Social

Studies/Science. With their help country's customs and manners, traditions, dresses, mode of living, fairs, festivals, political conditions, economic position etc. can be presented.

The development of international goodwill through its agency is highly psychological. Immediate events of international importance can easily be exhibited.

7. Film Strips. It refers to long strips on which many photographs, in a definite sequence are set. On this basis, the purpose of film strips can be fulfilled by showing slides in a continuous chain. Whatever the number of pictures drawn on film strip, those can be shown in a serial order with the help of the projector, so them a well planned manner, information may be available in a sequence, relating to concerned process or an event or the subject-matter. Any teacher with a little training can make pupils adapt. Its preparation is of the same type as that of a camera.

Film strips relating, to teaching in Social Studies/Science can be obtained from the libraries of concerned organisations. Professional centres also prepare such film strips and can be got from them.

8. Television. In modern age T.V. communication is a powerful medium. It involves auditory and visual organs. There is, a provision for recording the event and can be presented again and again. In India, with the help of the satellite; national programmes are being telecasted. These can be seen formally T.V. stations in the whole country. Programmes of other lands can also he seen in India.

To set the T.V. on, is easy. It needs no special kind of skill. To set it on and off, the indicators are there on the buttons. To use the T.V. in teaching, the teacher should follow the following steps:

> ***Preparation.*** For teaching in Social Studies/Science, the teacher should prepare himself. He should obtain needed material of all T.V. Centres and then be acquainted with all educational programmes. After his preparation, let him tell the pupils about the T.V. programmes and prepare them psychologically and mentally. After testing the T.V. it

should be brought before the pupils in the class. There should be proper sitting arrangement. The place of the T.V. should be in one corner out at eye level.

Presentation. The teacher should test the T.V. before it is shown to the pupils. There should be perfect discipline during the programme. Let pupils take down notes during this period. After the programme is over, the pupils be asked to complete their notes.

Follow up. There should be exchange of views on the subject of the programme. Let the pupils get their doubts removed. Pupils should be given opportunity to give a practical shape to the acquired knowledge There should be provision for evaluation of the programme.

Through T.V., teachers own development is possible. T.V. presents to pupils, models of excellence. High class artists and teachers are shown on the T.V. Through it, pupils are acquainted with realities of the world. It overcomes the deficiencies of good teachers and other equipment. With its help, the school can be developed as the community centre. T.V. makes education heap, and of high standard since expert teachers at the national level, are invited to the T.V. station. But, for this, the school time table should be adjusted to the T.V. programmes.

9. Video Tape or Audio-Video Cassettes. Along with the extension of the T.V., the use of video indicational and entertainment sphere, has increased. Its another name is Audio-Video Cassettes. In the domain of education this technology has cropped up as a movement which symbolises new dimensions and new symbols.

Now the pupil can, with the help of the Audio-Video Cassettes, receive education at home. Any event, lecture of the lesson can be got repeated as and when required. To revise a lesson may look bad, but not this one.

Its equipment needs the T.V. Video cassette *i.e.* video tapes on different topics are available which are prepared, of all courses by the N.C.E.R.T. and I.G.N.O.U. and are used in their study centres.

Utility in Teaching of Social Studies/Sciences

The invention of video technology is anew dimension. The Ministry of education has developed ET. in some subjects or areas. These can be seen with the help of the video camera. We can take shots of other scenes and with their help can present the same before the pupils. It infuses reality and life and the subject-matter can be presented to the pupils in a very effective manner which are as under:

1. Knowledge got through video is more lasting since the ears and eyes remain active.
2. These are very helpful in acquainting pupils with the industrial facts, and their impact, and of historical events and scientific researches.
3. Children who are low in intelligence and those who are high, on the one hand get entertainment and on the other hand receive all types of education.
4. Through good video tapes, the observation power and imagination of pupils can develop.
5. With these, the pupils can easily be given knowledge about situations and circumstances of various countries and about humanity.

MOTION PICTURES OR FILMS

Formerly motion pictures were thought to be meant for recreation and amusement only. Today they are increasingly used as a device of teaching. They are an indispensable means of education and instruction. Edison was so very enthusiastic about the utility of films as instruments of education that he once remarked, "The only text-book needed will be for the teacher's own use. Films will serve as guide posts to these teacher-instruction-books and not the books as guides to the films. Pupils will learn from films everything that is there in every grade from the lowest to the highest. Films are inevitable as practically the sole teaching method." However, the statement is an over estimate of the situation. A motion picture cannot be more than a visual aid. It may be used in any subject such as Social Studies where action is an important factor in giving a clear idea of the subject. In a film, the child can travel the long distances and move through centuries of time. He sets pictures of places, persons and activities which is impossible to obtain in other ways. Thus, motion pictures can reconstruct the past and bring the distant things in the classroom. They bring an element of realism into the classroom which cannot be obtained by any other medium of instruction. Slow-motion film is very useful from instructional point of view though it is not possible to skip over some scenes or to devote more attention to some and less to others. It is not possible to change the sequence as can be done in case of strips and slides.

Guidelines to Select and use Films in Social Studies

1. ***Relevant to the Unit or Topic of Study.*** Little learning will take place if a film is shown as an unrelated entertainment film.
2. ***Develop Concepts, Behaviour and Learning.*** For increased understanding of basic human activities which is the major aim of Social Studies instruction, the teacher should see that the film organises thinking around the basic concepts and aspects of human life. It should be able to develop the desirable aspects of human behaviour like co-operativeness, acceptance of responsibility, creativeness, and concern for others.
3. ***Improve Skills and Expression.*** Motion pictures illustrate process of communication skills and creative expression. Guided to discover such skills and processes pupils will improve their own skills and processes important in democratic living.
4. ***Suitable for Pupils for Whom it is used.*** The selected film should be suitable to the psychological development and social background of the pupils, for whom it is being used.
5. ***Accompanied by Follow-up Programmes.*** An educational film must be preceded by a proper preparation and succeeded by a proper follow-up. Careful selection of

films should be supplemented by a skilful follow-up in the form of general observations, comments or answers to specific questions, or general evaluation. The follow-up activities should be related to the aims and purposes, established for the use of the film. The pupils should be encouraged to enjoy and share the interesting features of the film.

Sources of Films

1. ***Universities and Departments of Education.*** Many universities and departments of education in different states, maintain good stock of educational films for colleges and schools.
2. ***Ministries.*** Films may be borrowed from the Ministry of Broadcasting, Ministry of Education and Publicity Department of States.
3. ***Pension Service Department and Audio-Visual Aids Department.*** These have been attached to various teacher training colleges throughout India. They lend films to schools in their own circle, free of any charges and hold regular refresher courses for school teachers for imparting training in the right use of audio-visual materials.
4. ***Embassies.*** Foreign Embassies also lend educational films to schools free of charge.

FILM STRIPS OR FILM SLIDES

A film-strip or film slide may be used as effectively as a motion picture. It consists of a series of still pictures, printed on strips of motion picture film, each of which is known as a frame. Film strips come in either the single frame or the double frame. They vary in length from about a foot to three or four feet. Unlike the motion pictures, they can be stopped and held with a single picture on the screen as long as needed. They are also more useful than motion pictures in terms of cost, availability, and use. Due to their low cost, schools can maintain their own film strip library. It is possible to discuss content of the film strip as it is being shown. Film strips are easy to catalogue and store and simple to show. Their production for use in the teaching of Social Studies, has increased greatly in recent year. Now many good strips are available on the various topics and units of Social Studies. Photographs, drawings, diagrams, paintings, written and printed matter are used as material for making a film strip. Coloured frames may be included at a small additional cost.

Advantages in Teaching Social Studies

1. ***A Good Readiness for Map Reading.*** Film strip also serves to introduce children to other countries of the world, showing how people in other lands live and work. Physical features of a particular area can be shown through a film strip in different Indian states.

2. ***Useful by Showing Development Features.*** Stages of development are a feature of the "movies" but for purpose of study and discussion can be shown in a series of stills. Film strips can profitably show what steps should be taken in an emergency such as fire, drowning, an accident and an air-raid etc. It may exhibit the history, growth and development of a particular area or how a letter reaches from one place to some other place, city or town.

3. ***Summarising.*** They may be profitably used to summarize learning and to re-emphasize important ideas at the end of a unit of study.

4. ***Preliminary use.*** Film strips is used at the initial stages of a unit to introduce a new topic or during the work-study stage for explanation and clarification.

5. ***Selected Materials.*** Film strips enable the teacher to show selected materials needed to discuss as the situation demands. Accompanied by recording some film strips require little or no commentary when they are being shown.

NEWSPAPERS

1. *Teaching Aid.* Daily newspapers are effective teaching aids to social studies. They motivate the children to know about past events. The pupil is interested in what is happening such as an, election or a recent invention. It is easy to lead him to the study of a election. Thus, newspapers serve as a motivational aid, for going from the known to the unknown, from the familiar to the unfamiliar.

2. *Starting Point.* Current happenings serve as a starting point to stimulate interest. Many news items utilize a unit and tie the past with the present. The study of newspaper reveals the relationship of specific events to the larger current scene.

3. *Resource.* Newspaper is a reservoir of resources and illustrations. It helps to clarify and exemplify the realities described in the text-books through contemporary occurrences. It may be used to augment other instructional resources. It is a means of sensitizing the class to the need for up-to-date information.

4. *Closing the Informational Gap.* Movements, trends, ideas and changes in politics and international relations. The space age inventions, discoveries, research and new developments in industries and significant scientific progress can help in closing the gap between information contained in the books and changing developments of the world. The special features, the editorials, cartoons, and advertisements enlighten the students. The special issues of newspapers—Republic Day Numbers, Industrial Supplements etc., are full of information. The life sketches of great personalities and the description of historical buildings and places enrich historical knowledge.

❐

5

Community Resources, Laboratory and Text-books

Every community has its own physical, social and cultural enviromnent, traditions, economic-natural resources and institution. All these community resources are available for occlusion in the Social Studies syllabus. The community is a type of laboratory for the school, which offers to pupils, first hand knowledge and experiences.

IMPORTANT COMMUNITY RESOURCES

Community is an imperishable store house of knowledge which is, there-in every form, available to pupils for contemplation and use. Temples, mosques, churches of the community, express the religious endeavours of the ancestors. In fact, it is all the result of efforts made by the community for spiritual satisfaction.

One of the important aims of Social Studies teaching is to produce useful, productive and effective citizens. Hence, it is necessary for the teacher to have full knowledge of his community resources and only then he can make his pupils earnest about their use. Under the guidance of the teacher, pupils will go to the community to collect required information, as they proceed to study and observe municipalities, news papers and periodicals, offices, public libraries, big and small industries. For this, the teacher can prepare effective subject lists of learning material, instruction/material to understand social life as whole.

M.P. Moffat is of the view, "Modern community with its available store of resources can assume the nature of a laboratory. The community life and the study of its activities as also the knowledge gained through the observation of complex social life, is very essential for education of the youth. Thus this practical knowledge is complimentary to the knowledge learnt in the class-room." The syllabus must be related to the problems of the community. Through its medium, pupils learn about men and their professions, trades, and industries, who create society or the community. He gets opportunities to talk about various aspects of the lives of persons. The experiences which the youth gets from his community, enhances his capability and offers him to look in present times, at the life, from wider angles.

While explaining the importance of the community, Moffat writes at one place, "Whatever may be the nature of the community, it has an important place in the education of the youth." The community enlivens and widens various types of learning and functions in the fond of a laboratory. It provides opportunities for various activities and their enjoyment, for utilising youths' leisure fruitfully. Various cultural resources of the community offer opportunities for their intellectual, expression and development. Pupils should have extensive knowledge of such resources. These resources are as under:

1. Historical Resources. This category includes ancient inscriptions-Historical works of the contemporary writers, autobiographies of greatmen, historical monuments, ancient Temples, the museum contain things excavated from places *e.g.* Ahad (Udaipur), Kalibanga, Mohen-jo-daro, Harappa etc. The history of these is closely related to the contemporary culture and civilisation. For this reason, all these things act as resources of social life.

2. Geographical Resources. These include geographical sites like different mountains, rivers, valleys, canals, means of transport, central ports, air buses, barages, tea gardens, big industrial undertaking, railways stations etc.

3. Government Institutions. The community includes municipalities, health centres, water works, fire brigade, police stations,

stations, secretariat, Sansad Bhawan, Judicial Courts, A.I.R. Stations, TV. Centres. Military stations, welfare centres.

4. Cultural Resources. Theatres, museums, libraries, cinema houses, zoo, art centre, T.V. centre, Bal Bhawan universities, ancient, buildings, forum, and other cultural resources are included.

5. Social Processes. Various items included are marriage ceremonies, festivals, fairs, customs and traditions, music and dancing etc. which can help in understanding Social Studies. Hence these can be used in giving practical form to effective teaching.

6. Scientific Resources. These sources include science libraries, hydro-electric generating centres, science centres, industrial centre, technical centre, National Scientific laboratories, computer and electronic centre and engineering colleges.

7. Economic Resources. These include, mandies, banks, dairies, business centres, milk plant, railway station, post and telegraph departmental offices, telephone exchanges, agricultural farms, printing press etc.

Hence community resources have unique place in respect of resources. We must make efforts to utilise its museums, libraries, art galleries, pilgrim centres, transport centres, recreations, trade, industrial, agricultural and science laboratories. These can be used in teaching social studies.

IMPORTANCE OF COMMUNITY RESOURCES IN THE TEACHING OF SOCIAL STUDIES

About the importance and uses of community resources, opinions of scholars are given below: "The aim of teaching Social Studies is to help the pupil to acquire knowledge of his environment, to develop power to understand human relations and some aptitudes and values which are essential for intelligent participation in matters relating to people, state, nation, and the world. –*Kothari Commission*

"Environment outside the class provides a natural laboratory. It presents to teachers and pupils extensive instructions relating to aids material. This is essential and becomes the basis of education of the youth through observation and instruction for leading life ill the complex society. *–Moffat*

Community resources can be used in two ways First, by bringing the community to the pupils and second by taking the school to the community.

BRINGING THE COMMUNITY NEARER TO STUDENTS

1. Invitation to Members of the Community. The schools should invite persons working in different sectors of the community life since it is very essential to give information regarding various areas. Doctors, social workers, lawyers businessmen, can give real knowledge by throwing light on various conditions of community life. Those coming from industrial spheres, can acquaint pupils with industrial problems. Doctor can give knowledge relating to causes and diagnosis, concerning his profession. In this way, by giving knowledge to pupils about different aspects of subjects, they can be prepared for shouldering community responsibilities.

2. Parent-Teacher Association. In order to make the school community centre, Parent-Teacher Association can be established. As a resource of the community, it can play an important role in the sphere of education as: *(a)* Parents may be invited to visit the school while teaching topics or units concerning the local community. They will present before the pupils, local facts relating to the unit/topic. *(b)* The school can collect information relating to the topic/unit by issuing questionnaire.

"The parent-teacher association can organise different meetings to bring teachers and pupils nearer to each other. In such meeting teachers and parents can exchange views on subjects of mutual interest." *–M.P.Moffat*

3. Film Shows, Exhibitions and Dramas. For the members of the community, the schools can arrange drama, film and exhibitions and thereby can attract the community to itself and can get its cooperation. These not only have entertainment value but educative value also.

4. Organisation of Different Activities. To bring the pupils nearer the community, the school should organise different activities pertaining to community life, so that the school can become successful as the community centre. Schools can organise different kinds of games sports, and competitions for the members of the community.

5. Solution of Community Problems. Pupils can be enabled to get the real knowledge of the community life through tackling community problems, Rural schools have their own several problems. The community people can render help in solving these problems.

6. Celebration of Festivals. The school can bring the pupils closer to the community by celebrating various festivals and local fairs, in the school complex inviting the community members.

TAKING THE SCHOOL NEARER TO THE COMMUNITY

In order to make the school, community centred and to bring it closer to the community, the teachers can make following efforts:

1. Organisation of Social Service Clubs/surveys. According to K.G.Saidain, "The teacher should organise social survey club in the school which may conduct investigation into immediate needs and problems of the community life *e.g.* condition of the roads, arrangement relating to sevage in the urban or rural areas conditions, in the neighbourhood, relating to health and sanitation, causes of spread of diseases etc." Survey of such type can be assigned to the group of pupils who have interest in the problem and the group should work under the guidance of the teacher. Projects, like this will give direct and first hand knowledge to the students relating to the enviroment in their neighbourhood.

2. Arrangement of Community Services. School is not there merely for giving knowledge. It is also necessary to cultivate right thoughts and attitudes in children. Along with book knowledge, practical knowledge related to the community, is very necessary, since the child lives in the community. Education is futile if he does not understand the problems of the community and is not inspired inwardly to solve them. Even otherwise, "Learning by doing"is considered as the best from psychological point of view. Community service projects offer to pupils opportunities to learn.

3. Trips and Tours. For providing knowledge, trips and tours can be arranged. Through this medium pupils can observe local conditions. The school can organise different kinds of trips—short, general and extensive ones.

The Kothari Commission has suggested additional fourth element, known as 'Service.' Service sense creates in pupils good qualities and outlooks, While serving the community through social service projects, pupils acquire several new experiences. When pupil gets experiences through sense, these become stable all the more. These lead to their alround development. National Service Scheme which has been adopted in all the colleges in the country, is the best course for developing service sense. In schools too, such activities can be started as cleanliness in the school, looking after garden etc. In the same way pupils can adopt some such projects outside the school. This will offer to pupils opportunities to meet members of the community outside the four walls of the school and besides recreation, they will get real knowledge. Pupils can take up some such community projects, as:

1. Tree plantation
2. Sanitation in the rural and urban areas.
3. Adult Education
4. Family Planning
5. Purifying Wells etc.

In this way, several other projects can be adopted by the schools, but the following points must be kept in mind, while adopting any project:

(a) The project should have academic importance since, when he comes to the school, his primary aim is to receive education. So, there should be educational aim behind every activity carried out in the school.

(b) Projects should be such as to benefit the community.

(c) Projects should be taken in hand when pupils have adequate time at disposal *e.g.* in the evening they can take up the task in the community or during holidays.

(d) Projects should be according to the age, and mental level of the pupils.

(e) Projects should not be tough and costly.

Through these programmes the community can come nearer to schools and vice versa. Owing to such mutual relations they are enabled to function for the welfare of each other. M.P. Moffat says, "Secondary school is a chief social resource and will play an important role in the future set-up of the community. Enlightened and active people, can help a lot in meeting the needs and solving problems of the community."

So, in the end, we can say that on mutual cooperation between schools and the community, the existence of both is secured. For this, the teachers play an important role If the teachers happen to be men of character, expert in their subjects, offering sympathetic treatment to children and will also keep in mind, the interests of the community, then the members of the community, themselves will be attracted towards them and will cooperate with them. At the same time, having understood the difficulties of the community, teachers should cooperate.

UTILISATION COMMUNITY RESOURCES

We have already explained in the answer to the first question that community resources can be used in two ways: *(i)* To take the school to the community; *(ii)* To take the community to the school.

(A) Bringing School Nearer to Community

1. ***Excursion.*** Excursion and tours should be included in planned educational experiences. Through direct observational Pupils knowledge about problems of community increases and their ideas become crystal clear. In rural areas, and community have intimate contact. So, excursion of the type enables pupils to be familiar with the flora and fauna of the region. In addition, they get opportunities to see for themselves, irrigational facilities, roads, highways, production from land, cottage industries, trade and peoples' economic life in direct form and can easily have knowledge about the rural life and environment. In the same way the pupils from rural areas can be taken to cities to see factories, power houses, mills, bank, railway junction, aerodrome, cinema halls, radio station, historical buildings, mansions, schools, colleges, universities, zoo, museum and other such things.

2. *Community Survey.* For educative experiences, pupils can conduct several types of surveys. But in order to be useful, correct information must be collected. Any aspect of history, economic conditions, social institutions, customs and traditions of the community can be studied. Surveys can also be conducted to study the problems of the community. After collecting data, tables may be framed to understand the structure and processes of the community, by carrying out analysis. Such surveys, develop the outlook of the pupils and they get training for creative participation in solving social problems. These impart training in democratic citizenship. Cooperation and tolerance develop in them and through interaction, they develop sense of belongingness to the community.

The school can obtain, through survey, knowledge about any aspect of the community. For example, past history of a region, social institutions, customs and manners, practices, folk tales and folk songs and community problems like cleanliness, employment etc. These are some problems which if surveyed, can cultivate interest in pupils.

(B) Bringing Community Nearer to Schools

1. *Parent-teachers Association.* Every school should have this type of association. When parents, as members of this association, visit the school, they, will understand, about the interests, aptitudes, and peculiarities of character, of their own children. Teachers will also know about the general needs of the community and the community will be able to observe functioning of the school.

2. *Inviting Different Personalities for Delivering Lectures.* Some special people from the community, who are attached with various professions and activities, should also be invited in the school from time to time. These persons will be able to tell pupils, at length, about their important activities and about various kinds of community services. In the same way persons coming from other cities, state or from abroad, should also be invited to deliver lecture lathe pupils, so as to give general information relating to the life of people in their own cities, state and foreign countries.

3. *Discussion on Important National and International Subjects.* Eminent leaders, special personalities should be invited in the school from time to time to speak on important current problems like national integration and international understanding and local people should also be invited to attend such functions.

4. *Social Service Activities.* Different kinds of social services can be organised in the school *e.g.* adult education programme can be conducted by pupils and teachers in the evening. In the same way the school can run a small dispensary or a library for the benefit of the community. By organising social services, the school can impart to pupils, practical knowledge of the Social Studies subject.

5. *Celebration of Fairs and Festivals.* In the school, camps can be organised. Functions like that of the Repubtic Day, Independence Day, U.N.O. Day and Fundamental Rights Day and martyrs days, both days of great men, can be celebrated. Local persons can be invited to participate in these functions. Exhibitions can also be organised for the benefit of the community. Red Cross week or blood donation camp can be organised. In addition, local people can be invited on the occasions of the annual prize distribution function, parents day, annual sports, dramatics, exhibitions, political recitations etc.

The above cited activities will not only enhance school and community relationship, but will also relate education with life. This sort of programme includes, sanitation, approach road, water supply etc. These will cast definite impact on pupils and will mean self service through social service. It is the only form in which school can certainly become community school *i.e.*, of the community, for the community and by the community.

NEED AND IMPORTANCE OF SOCIAL STUDIES/SCIENCE LABORATORY

Need. A separate class or laboratory is necessary for the teaching of Social Studies/Science because without it the Social Studies teacher will experience difficulty in moving essential audio-visual aids from one place to another. So, if these be a special room for this subject, then all equipments can be arranged in it. In case the social studies room is equipped with desired furniture, maps, charts, models, projector and other audio-visual aid it creates a motivating environment for the study of this subject. A classroom with such an atmosphere, assume the fond of a laboratory, in which all work is based upon the activities and the participation of the pupils who feel interested, get facilities and are inspired to work.

In the modem instruction methods, the use of text-book method or lecture method is not sufficient But problem method, project method, source method, socialised methods and other progressive teaching methods are utilised. For using these methods, it is necessary that the social studies class is specially set and particular kind of equipment may be there. This can be done only in a social room.

Importance. In the above account it is clear that in modern age, the need for laboratory in teaching of Social Studies/Science is increasing, because:

1. ***Continuation of the Subject.*** While introducing Social Studies, quite often it becomes necessary to draw big diagram pictures. The teacher having laboured hard in one period, prepare these pictures and as soon as the period ended the next subject teacher entered and robbed off these lines and diagram. Due to this, whatever was taught by Social Studies/Science teacher all labour becomes wasteful. Had there been a separate Social Studies room, or laboratory, he could have preserved these pictures and diagrams and could have presented them to pupils every time while teaching the subject.

2. ***Variety in the Subject.*** The nature of Social Studies/ Science teaching methods is changing in modern times. Modern teacher does not depend only on lecture and text-book methods but makes use of other facilities which are essential for good work. There are text-books, manual, newspapers periodicals, maps, globe, chart and other equipments, which introduce variety in the subject and attract pupils.

3. ***Saving Energy and Time.*** Teaching of Social Studies/ Science does not remain confined only to class-room, but need for some activities, and as such it is necessary to convert the class-room itself, into a laboratory. Because to bring the equipment from the store and after teaching, to restore the same back, involves a good deal of wastage of time. Energy is lost. These can be saved if laboratory is there.

   In the past, the geography room was used for the purpose. The fact was that these subjects were taught in open space. The people had the presumption, that these subjects could be taught by any person and for doing this, no specific ability was required. Now Social Studies has becomes a dynamic subject. Only a resourceful teacher can make his teaching effective. But, however efficient a teacher may be without proper atmosphere, he cannot make learning exciting. So, as in the case of science subjects, there should be a separate room for laboratory, for teaching Social Studies, to contain all equipments concerned with Social Studies. Social Studies room should have a variety of equipments *e.g.* charts, maps, outline, drawing, globe etc. Hence, because of steady increase in the teaching aids, the Social Studies room came to called a laboratory. "In modern education, the class-room has become a learning laboratory, and greater emphasis is placed on students activities and participation in class-room procedures.

4. ***Real Knowledge.*** Social Studies/Science is an integrated subject, comprising history, geography, political science, economic, sociology etc. Hence to impart to pupils real knowledge relating to historical events, geographical conditions, political, economic, sociology conditions, forest wealth, mineral wealth, means of transport and communication, power and water resources, can be given with the help of aids placed in the laboratory.
5. ***Environment.*** There is no proper environment for teaching. Social Studies/Science if taught in an ordinary room, but if it is done in a laboratory, the pupils and teachers will be more inspired to work, since the environment is suitable for this.
6. ***Achievements of Good Results.*** If for teaching of Social Studies/ Science, laboratory is available; good results can be obtained, most certainly, since in laboratory, the pupil can suitably utilise his interest, aptitude and resourcefulness. This develops self confidence in pupils.

Set-up of Social Studies/Science Laboratory

By assigning responsibilities to the pupils in a class-room laboratory it is possible to cultivate good relations among pupils and teachers. As far as possible, allot some responsibility or another to all pupils for a specified duration of time. At the commencement of the acadamic session, committees should be constituted for collecting and distributing equipment which may help the teacher in various ways and let some pupils be its chairman. An arrangement of this sort, develops collective leadership and active cooperation in pupils, which is very essential and useful for a democratic society. These committees/societies may be as follows: *(i)* For selecting and purchasing books, periodicals. *(ii)* To organised pictures and equipment, *(iii)* To set-up bulletin board, *(iv)* For arranging recreational programmes, *(v)* To contact big institutions and persons.

EQUIPMENT OF SOCIAL STUDIES/SCIENCE LABORATORY

The following equipment is essential for Social Studies/Science laboratory:

(1) Chalk-Board. These need not necessarily be black, but can be green, white, yellow or of any colour. Every room must have one or more chalk-boards, since without chalk-board, no Social Studies room can be called complete. These can be used for writing summary of the lesson, for sketching outline diagrams. These should generally be facing the class and placed at such a place, to enable all pupils to see what is put on the board. Chalk pieces of different colours can also-be used on these boards.

(2) Furniture. The laboratory should have fifty to sixty comfortable chairs and tables. The aims and methods of the present-day education are fast changing. Today, the pupils have to carry out deliberations and critical study which require organising symposia and seminars. Hence to use all methods of teaching, proper arrangement will have to be made, removing tables and chairs if not required. So, the tables should be light and the size and height of the chairs should suit the pupils. Almirahs should also be there to shelf books.

(3) Bulletin Board. It can be used for any purpose. It should be placed in the corridor of the room of Social Studies/Science laboratory. The teacher can use it for giving information, relating to instruction in the subject. Secondly, it can be used for displaying diagrams/sketches prepared by pupils and also the cuttings and clippings for the newspapers/periodicals, so as to acquaint the pupils with the daily happenings.

(4) Cabinet and Files. To stock various types of equipments, racks, files, stands and shelves should be made available as required. After fishing their tasks pupils may keep all their articles in the cabinet and files. These should be affixed with relevant tables. Keeping these cabinets and files in cases or spaces, will facilitate the locating of necessary equipment.

(5) Light. Work by pupils, in dark rooms, casts unhealthy effect on their vision and they get exhausted. So, there should be adequate arrangement of light and air in the Social Studies laboratory and should be white wash in pleasing colours. As for as possible every Social Studies room should be sound proof so that neither the noise from outside comes in and nor the voices of the pupils engaged in practical work in the Social Studies room go outside or to other rooms.

(6) Audio-Visual Aids. Only that will be called an experimental laboratory in Social Studies, which is equipped with different kinds of audio-visual aids. This kind of equipment includes pictures, maps, globe, charts, commercial cartoons, timelines, specimens, films and film strips, radio, tape recorder, projector etc.

(7) Essential Equipment and Machines. All instruments to be used by pupils, such as, for the study of geography, barometer, thermometer, hydrometer, weather cock etc. should be there in the laboratory of this subject. National Flags of different countries can also be displayed. Such an equipment included colours/dyes, water colours, coloured pencils, ink pen, brush, tape, scissors, knife, different coloured-papers, gum, needles, drawing-set, nails etc.

After equipping Social Studies/Science laboratory, besides regular periods in Social Studies, some periods in the week should be set aside for practical work in the laboratory. The main purpose of this is to develop skills, abilities and creative expression. In these periods, the pupils are engaged m preparing maps, graphs, charts, timelines, models, pictures, solving problems, to tackle projects, to find out answer to questions or to do assignments, individually or collectively. For assignments, pupils should be given specific instructions and be told clearly from where can they get the required equipment. Pupils, researchers should be given full freedom to move the laboratory to make full use of the equipment. In these practical periods, the teacher functions only as a guide and/or to supervise. This type of laboratory work develops fine relations between the teacher and the taught because they work together and continue to learn simultaneously. In the laboratory, the feeling remains that they all are engaged in such an activity, even though working, individually or collectively.

LIBRARY OF SOCIAL STUDIES/SCIENCE

Library is a laboratory for tackling the problem of individual differences. On the one hand, it becomes the centre for displaying, maps, drawing pupils work, on the other hand it can become a collection of films, artistic things, specimens, models, etc. So, the library is an index of pupils sentiments and achievements. In it, all pupils can study, according to facilities and their aptitudes. Books relating to all aspects of Social Studies as stated below, should be available in the library /laboratory.

1. **Reference Books.** These cover, dictionaries, encyclopaedeas, year books, atlas, gazette, source books, special reference tools. These should be of there in Social Studies library. Pictorial encyclopaedea will be very-beneficial for pupils.
2. **Books.** According to Wasley, "The Social Studies library should have books on beasts, birds., fairies, dramatics, stories, arts, biographies, trade and industry, urban and rural life, research, valour, burning events, offences, family life, diet, friendship, health, hobbies, administration, literatures or other countries, social problems, professions etc."
3. **Books on Related Subjects.** It should contain some good books on various curricular subjects which can be utilised as and when needed.
4. **Books Dealing with Development.** Those dealing with various levels of development should be there in the library.
5. **Recreational Books.** In Social Studies library recreational books should also find place so that pupils learn use their leisure time properly.
6. **Professional Books.** These should be there according to the needs and interests of the teachers.

TEXT-BOOKS

Text-book of Social Studies is the fundamental tool for teaching Social Studies. It is an aid which is accessible to both a teacher and a student . As in the past and so it the present all education in Indian school is book centred. A teacher follows it closely in order to perform the duty of finishing the syllabus.

Need and Place of Social Studies Text-Book

The traditional way of using books as sources of knowledge has many dangers, yet, there is a need and place of text-book of social studies in our school because:

1. ***It Helps to Proceed from the Concrete to the Abstract.*** Knowledge is power only when it is used and for using it one needs assimilation. Knowledge is to be remembered and applied. For this, the students should keep notes which is not possible because he is too young to keep records or take down notes and at the same time listen to what the teacher is teaching. It is because of this, there arises the need of a good text-book in Social Studies.
2. ***Social Studies is a New Subject.*** Social Studies is a new subject in the curriculum and good text-books on this subject are not available. It is not possible for a student of high school to correlate geography with history and economics nor has he a keen observation to study and observe the local community and its social customs. He cannot understand as to how this society has come into being in its present form and how to interpret intelligently the matrix of social forces. Even the Social Studies teachers are groping in the dark. Therefore, for the guidance of teachers as well as students, good text-books in Social Studies are need. They need a text-book which have been written round topic, themes, movement and social problems. Students and teachers need text-books written according to concept, aims and objectives and which include latest information in social sciences.

Role of a Social Studies Text-Book

Needed by Average Teacher. A good teacher will certainly like to draw up his own scheme of studies as well as notes and exercises.

But every teacher is not expected to be equal to the task nor our education system allows him this freedom. It is here that the need of a good-book arises in teaching a subject like Social Studies.

A Social Studies is a new subject in the curriculum. Suitable text-books are not yet available in good number. Therefore, either separate books written on history, geography and civics or bulky volume of books on Social Studies containing topics from history, geography and civics combined together are be used. As they are not written according to the true concept of Social Studies such books are of little use. Their authors have never thought that Social Studies is a compact whole whose object is to adjust the students to their social environment so that they may be able to understand how society has come to its present form and how to interpret the matrix of social forces and movements in the midst of which they are living. Good text-books on Social Studies, written round topics, themes, movements or problems, are essential for their guidance of teachers. The main basis of Social Studies instruction has to be the text-book, written according to the concept, aims and objectives of this new subject.

CRITERIA OF A GOOD TEXT-BOOKS

1. **Child-centred.** Related to the daily life of the pupils, a good text-book on Social Studies should be suitable to the age, ability and interests of the pupils for whom it is written.
2. **Well-illustrated.** It should be illustrated with pictures, charts, diagrams, time-lines, sketches, graphs and maps to make the subject-matter clear and easily understandable and to sustain the interest of pupils.
3. **Logical and Systematic Treatment of Topics.** Social Studies is a vast subject drawing its material from various sources to reveal children where they are in time, space and society and relationship which links the present with the past, the local with the distant and personal and national life with the life and cultures of people living in other lands. Only a subject-matter arranged under topics, systematically

and logically will give them a clear idea of the development of human civilization in its various aspects.

4. **Full of useful Experiences and Exercises.** Teaching of Social Studies aims at the development of skills and attitudes besides acquisition of knowledge. To achieve this aim situations should be created through suggested problems, exercises and activities and students should be given actual experiences in those situations.
5. **Simple and Clear Language.** Long and difficult sentences or words should not be used in a Social Studies text-book. Its vocabulary should be well-selected, easy and forceful. Its style should be straight-forward and not involved. It should be free from misprint and other mistakes. Technical words should be explained fully with adequate examples.
6. **Suggesting Good Methods of Learning.** Subject-matter of Social Studies should be presented along with its suggested its application. It should give practical suggestions for applying the knowledge gained through the construction of models, organisation of visits and field trips and the preparation of charts, maps and other illustrations. A brief summary should be given at the end of each chapter along with exercises, containing questions to be attempted independently at home by students.
7. **Free from Bias.** A good text-book should-inspire high ideas of human brotherhood, communal harmony and international understanding. It should present the truth with academic freedom. The authors of text-books should not attempt to promote their personal points of view, ignoring facts and truths.
8. **Accurate.** The statements made in the text-book should be absolutely true though, telling the truth about social sciences like history, economics, sociology or political science, is a difficult task. The facts should be given as supported by evidence.

9. **Constant Modification and Revision.** The Social Studies text-book should be kept upto-date as regards its subject-matter, through revision and modification each year according to the latest development in life and environment. It must contain latest information of all the aspects of national life.

10. **Satisfactory Get-up.** The cover of the text-book should be artistic and appealing. The size of the print and the quality of paper should be upto the mark. The text-book should be well-bound, durable and lasting for a pretty long time.

Proper use of Text-Books

1. ***Reference Purpose of the Text-Book.*** It should serve only as a book of reference for both the teacher and the pupil. It should supplement teaching and not supplant it. A teacher who depends too much on a text-book, leaves a bad impression upon the pupil's mind, both about himself and the subject. He should supplement it with the subject-matter from other text-books, references and resources.

2. ***Varying Approaches.*** There should be varying approach of different authors to clarify the same point and to give a wider range of knowledge.

3. ***Teacher's Additions.*** The teacher should also make additions with material of his own. His subject is not a finished product. It should be ever-developing and ever-reviewing itself. A text-book should be an instrument in his hands. He should not be an instrument of the text-book.

4. ***Determining the Sequence of Contents.*** The teacher should determine the sequence of contents that will suit best his purpose in the beginning of the year.

5. ***Developing a Readiness for Each Unit.*** This requires some class discussion, map work, story telling or similar activities, which "set the stage" for the main part of the book to be undertaken.

6. ***Introduction to Contents.*** In the beginning pupils should be introduced to the contents of the entire book, along with its special features. This will give them an idea of the complete programme of Social Studies and build up a general readiness for the work of the entire year.
7. ***Stimulate.*** This Social Studies text-book should be used to stimulate a spirit of enquiry, in accordance with the abilities and interests of the pupils and according to availability of sources.
8. ***Proper use of Questions and Exercises at the End of the Unit.*** Given at the end of each unit or chapter the text-book exercises should be studied by the teacher for providing more challenging work to one or two selected groups of pupils and for revision work for the rest of the class.

Advantages of a Good Text-Book

1. ***Meeting the Needs of Students.*** Written from students' point of view, recognising their difficulties and limitations, a good text-book meets their requirements by the use of simple language, headings, sub-headings, questions, exercises, maps, charts, pictures and other illustrative aids.
2. ***Developing Study Skills.*** Providing a common basis on which the process of reading, analysing, outlining and summarising can be mastered, a good text-book furnishes a common laboratory in which study skills can be developed.
3. ***Suggesting Application of the Material Read.*** Not only giving the required subject-matter, a good text-book also suggests application of that material through assignments, drills, questions, projects, problems and other exercises of all sorts—reproductive, imaginative, dramatic and manual.
4. ***Giving the Accurate Account of the Subject.*** Giving a reasonable correct account of the subject, field or area in an organised manner the treatment of the subject-matter in a good text-book is logical and systematic and according to

the latest syllabus, prescribed for the class. It sets a standard of the minimum essential for the students of all categories in the class.

5. ***Reflecting and Establishing Standards.*** Indicating what a teacher is required to teach and what a pupil is expected to learn, a good text-book affects methods and reflects the standards of scholarship.
6. ***Serving as a Basis for All the Methods.*** Suggested in the text-book at the end of each chapter Assignment Procedure or Discussion, Problem, Project and Unit methods can all be used with advantage with the help of a text-book.
7. ***Expanding and Limiting its Scope and Size According to Needs.*** Expanding and delimiting its scope, size and content according to the changing requirements of education a good text-book may lead and sometimes follow the educational process.

❐

6

Teacher and Lesson Planning

As Social Studies is a new-comer, in the school curriculum, very few people understand its true nature. More than any other subject, it demands well prepared and conscientious men and women of sound knowledge and good training, to teach it. In addition to the prescribed subject-matter, the teacher is also required to deal with attitudes, skills and appreciations. He is expected to produce intelligent citizens and responsible leaders. He has to handle the raw human material and transform it into well-adjusted, well-informed and happy citizens who will successfully participate in matters of national and international importance. He is, thus, the real, "architect of nation". Pointing to Social Studies teacher H. G. Wells remarked: "The teacher is the real maker of history." He is a substitute of the parent; a friend, a guide and a true master.

Functions of Social Studies Teacher

1. ***Gathering Knowledge of Education and Child Psychology.*** Knowing the nature, needs interests, capacities and limitations of his pupils Social Studies teacher will be able to provide for the effective growth of his pupils, during the formative years of their life. He must know each child well and treat each child individually and with understanding. As a good teacher he understands that learning is a continuous process through the active participation of the

child, he is more a counsellor, a guide, a co-worker and a friend than a mere teacher.

2. ***Gathering Knowledge of the Social Sciences and of Current Affairs.*** A Social Studies teacher draws his national form. Therefore he must know them well. He should, also keep himself in touch with the current affairs to utilize this material for supplementing Social Sciences and for facilitating instruction. As good text-books on Social Studies are scarcely available, the Social Studies teacher should be a well-informed, alert, fair-minded and a communicative person.

3. ***Interpretation and Connection between Different Groups and Elements.*** While discussing the functions of a Social Studies teacher Mr.M.L. Jacks states in his book *"Total Education"* "Above all he is an interpreter—interpreting not only the experiences of his pupils but also the community to which they belong, its past no less than its present, its purposes and its efforts to achieve those purposes, its cultural and technical achievements, its opportunities and possibilities, the invitations to service which it extends and the rewards, glittering or dimly discovered which it offers". The Social Studies teacher can interpret the school to the community, the community to the school, the teachers to the parents and the parents to the teachers. He is in an ideal position to explain the past in terms of the present and the present in terms of the past. He can, bring together the past and the present, the new and the old, the alien and the native, the near and the distant.

4. ***Selecting and Arranging Topics for Instruction in Social Studies.*** Though material from history, geography, economics and civics is, available, the historian's history, the geographer's geography and the economist's economics cannot serve the purpose of social studies without revision,

simplification and reorganisation. Social Studies teacher draws only the functional material from Social sciences. He logically arranges it into suitable units for his pupils. Books on Social Studies written according to the syllabus, prescribed by the authorities may be available but these cannot replace the teacher as the books do not keep in view the capacities and interests of different groups of pupils.

Qualities of a Social Studies Teacher

The success or failure of any educational programme depends upon the quality of instruction. Besides courses of study, reading material, equipment and good spacious class-rooms, good supervision and administration also contribute to the success and effectiveness of instruction. All these factors are ineffective without a good teacher who possesses certain qualities of head and heart. To quote Sir John Adams, "If the teacher is to prove really a maker of man, he must possess qualities of personality, character and intellect". However, the teacher has got his own limitations. All the teachers of Social Studies may not possess all the required qualities but they should try to equip themselves with the maximum possible qualities in spite of their own limitations.

1. *Physical Qualities*

(i) Good Personal Appearance. A teacher should have a good personal appearance to produce good impression upon those who come in his contact. Free from all physical deformities and abnormalities, he should be neither too tall nor too short, neither too fleshy nor too lean, neither too black nor too white. He should be a normal human being having tolerable features, smart, clever and active. A shabbily dressed, untidy and bad-looking teacher is seldom liked and owned by the pupils.

(ii) Clear and Pleasant Voice. A social studies teacher should possess a clear appealing voice, neither too low nor unnecessarily loud and shrill. Regular practice and care can

make his voice effective and appealing. He should neither shout in the class nor speak too fast. Clear in his speech he should be audible to all of his pupils, sitting in different corners of the class-room.

(iii) *Good Physical Health.* Physical health brings smartness, enthusiam, vigour, vitality, and activeness, so essential for a Social Studies teacher. Good physical health will make the teacher alert, cheerful and emotionally stable enabling him to meet the day-to-day demands of a modern school. A sound mind can live only in a sound body. A sound body requires regularity and moderation of habits, simple nourishing diet, participation in sports and games and physical exercise.

2. *Moral Qualities*

(i) *Friendliness, Sympathy and Understanding.* A good teacher should be the best friend and guide of his pupils. Sympathetic, kind hearted and humane towards his pupils he must understand their difficulties and problems and try to remove them. As pupils look to him for guidance and encouragement at every step, he must exhibit deep interest in them, in their activities, their welfare and their progress in studies.

(ii) *Honesty, Sincerity and Impartiality.* Absolutely fair in his dealings with others, a good teacher must be just, honest and impartial and free from all prejudices and bias. To win respect from others his words must reflect his actions. As M.K.Gandhi said, "Woe to the teacher who teaches one thing with the lips and carries another in the heart." Not the teacher's words, but his actions carry weight with the young students.

3. *Psychological Qualities*

(i) *Tactullness, Patience and Self-control.* A good Social Studies teacher should do the right thing at the right moment, even under trying circumstances. He should be able to skilfully control the young children under his charge. He must keep cool and balanced. He should exhibit patience and control of nerves even if things are not happening according to his wishes and expectations. Patience is required not only dealing with own pupils but also with officials senior colleagues, publicmen and common people.

(ii) *A sense of Humour.* "The class-room has no place for a confirmed pessimist and long faced, sour-visaged and humourless grouch. The class-room needs to be a happy place and it cannot be that without a good-natured teacher in charge." Therefore a good teacher should possess a sense of humour to delight his pupils in tense moments. A good laugh will relax pent-up feelings and exhausted nerves and will, thus, pave a way for further action and concentrated efforts.

(iii) *Sound Mental Health.* A dejected, frustrated, melancholic and pessimist teacher cannot create wholesome influence upon his pupils. He must always be cheerful and optimist and have faith in the goodness of humanity. Whatever may be the conditions and circumstances in which he is put, he must adjust himself to those environments. This is possible only when he possesses emotional stability and control over his anger and passions.

4. *Social Qualities*

(i) *Faith in World Citizenship.* Social Studies teacher should have faith that international co-operation is desirable and possible. An integrated individual he should be skilled in the art and science of human behaviour, conscious of the wide variety of behaviour patterns in the world to which he may have to adjust. He should know the goals of education for international understanding. He should be fully conversant with methods and resources for such programmes.

(ii) *Faith in Democracy.* A social studies teacher should be an example of democratic values. He should act as a democratic group leader and create environment for the reconstruction of experience, utilizing many school library and community resources. Organising democratic groups which widen the area of common concern encourage social interaction and guide democratic specialisation, he should have find faith in freedom, justice, equality and fraternity in his dealings with others.

5. *Executive Qualities*

(i) *Initiative and Resourcefulness.* A good teacher should be able to collect material and adopt his plans according to the circumstances. He should be sensible enough to take independent action in case of emergency as and when the occasion demands. Without running to the Headmaster or to other superior officers, he should be able to fare problems, think of their solution and then try to solve them to the best of his ability.

(ii) *Organising and Directive Capacity.* As an organiser, the social studies teacher should be able to put his plans into a workable form. For a job to be done in the best possible manner and with the least wastage of time, money and energy. He should select the most competent person for doing a job for which he or she is best fitted and in which he or she is genuinely interested. He should chalk out plans and prepare a framework before hand to facilitate the desired educational programme. As a leader and a director, he must be a person of wisdom and vision, with a thorough knowledge of facts.

6. *Scholarship.* Scholarship is not only desirable but essential for a successful Social Studies teacher, the subject, he is required to teach, is very vast and extensive. He may be face to face with many problems, if his own knowledge is not broader than the subject-matter that he teaches. In ancient India a teacher was held in high esteem in society because of his scholarship and high degree of learning the Social Studies teacher must have:

(i) A Sound Knowledge of the Subject-matter. A Social Studies teacher must know his subject well enough and deep enough. To have a broad and thorough knowledge of the content fields .to enable him to select material for his subject according to his needs. He must be a specialist in at least two of the Social Sciences such as history, geography, economics, political science and sociology.

(ii) Originality. A regular reader of books, newspapers, periodicals and magazines etc. should keep his knowledge thorough and up-to-date. Social Studies teacher should not be contented only by what others say but should be in a position to form his own independent judgement of men and affairs. He should have a habit of enquiry and scientific approach, desire for truth and spirit of independence, and initiative and originality to face any class-room situation that may arise unexpectedly

(iii) A Background of General and Liberal Education. The social studies teacher must be broad and of varied interests. He must apply his mind in as many subjects and activities as possible. He should have a keen interest in current affairs, an appreciation for the dominant role of science in human life and a habit of approaching social problems with the scientific method of enquiry. He should be able to explain the present in relation to the past correctly and successfully. He should keep himself very well-informed about all the happenings and general problems concerning men and affairs.

7. *Professional Background.* Professional background is also essential for successful teaching. Professional background includes:

(i) *Professional Attitude.* A real teacher is not a person who merely takes up a teaching job. He becomes a teacher by his faith and mental attitude. Possessing a natural aptitude for this profession, he takes to teaching, not because nothing else was available to him to make both ends meet, but because he was fired with the ambition of serving humanity through a vocation of his own liking and interest. He looks upon his work as a sort of dedication and mission not as a job or profession.

(ii) *Desire for Improvement.* Teaching is a progressive occupation A teacher must always be a student. Although this is true of all teachers, it is especially true of a Social Studies teacher who has to keep pace with all the changes in philosophies and techniques of education and rapid changes in physical, political and social environment of man. He must keep himself abreast of the latest development through regular study of books, newspapers, journals and magazines etc. He must be able to understand the perplexing problems of present-day world in their true context. He should know that education is dynamic and not static. He should always strive for improvement. Besides reading latest books and magazines on education, he should also attend seminars, refresher courses meetings, conferences, and work-shops on this subject, held in each state under Extension Services Department, attached to Teachers Training Colleges.

(iii) *Processional Training.* A good teacher must undergo professional training as teaching is both an art and a science. Like all other technical professions teaching requires sound professional training. A Social Studies teacher must, attend a full course of training in a teachers training college. During which he will study effective methodical procedures as well as proper use of audio-visual aids. He will also study child psychology to understand the chief mental and physical characteristics of the various stages of the child's development.

8. *Good Relationship*

(i) Relationship With Pupils. To command faith, loyalty and respect a teacher must take genuine interest in his pupils. He must mix with them, play with them, participate in various activities and encourage them on all occasions. He must pay individual attention towards the backward, abnormal and problem students.

(ii) Relationship with Community. A teacher should feel himself responsible to the whole society. The school is an agency that society has set up to instruct its young members. He, therefore, has an obligation to the parents of his pupils and to the community at large. As both home and school are engaged in a cooperative task we must, welcome contacts and conferences with parents on various occasions in the interest of the education of this pupils.

(iii) Relationship with Colleagues. The teacher must cultivate intimate relationship. With other members of the staff he must always be obliging and co-operating. He must give his colleagues a helping hand whenever required. He must neither backbite nor unnecessarily interfere in their affairs. He should work closely with the administration and be obedient and loyal. He should, enjoy academic freedom, but not do anything that will reflect upon his position as a teacher.

LESSON PLANNING

The word meaning of 'lesson planning' means to plan to lesson so as to attain educational objectives. The teaching process has to pass through three phases:

(a) Pre-active phase

(b) Inter-active phase

(c) Post-active phase

The lesson planning is concerned with pre-active phase of teaching. In this phase, the teacher has to plan different activities relating to teaching. So, in simple words, to write down systematically all those activities which he will carry out in the class to attain instructional objectives, is known as lesson planning.

According to N.L. Bossin, "Lesson-plan is the title given to a statement: of achievements to be realised and the specific means by which these are attained as a result of activities engaged during the period."

According to Davis, "Lesson plan must be prepared before going to the class, for there is nothing so fatal to a teacher's progress as unpreparedness."

In brief, we can say that careful planning of lesson is essential for good teaching. Ryburn said, "To teach, we must use experiences already gained as starting point of our work."

As in other subjects, in teaching Social Studies too, the teacher must keep in mind the following facts:

(i) To state the objectives of teaching in broad terms.

(ii) After stating broad teaching objectives, those should be precisely deemed and specified in behavioural terms.

(iii) To organise the subject matter for realising set objectives.

(iv) To arrange re-inforcement, for evaluation of teaching learning.

NEED AND IMPORTANCE OF LESSON PLANNING

Lesson planning is necessary for successful teaching. The lesson plan covers, the sort of questions to be asked to arouse curiosity of pupils, and to overcome their difficulties. So, with pre-planning, he finds himself capable of achieving aims of teaching adequately. The following is the importance and the need of lesson planning.

1. ***Organisation of Subject-Matter.*** For achieving the set objectives it is necessary to organise the subject-matter.

The importance of lesson planning is there for presenting the subject-matter and its evaluation.

2. ***Knowledge of Teaching Activities.*** Before writing the lesson plan the teacher decides teaching activities and how to use teaching aids.

3. ***Clarity of Teaching Objectives.*** For the clarity of objectives of teaching, he does not waste time by going astray. It is because the objectives will be clear.

4. ***Organised Knowledge.*** It is necessary to present the knowledge to the pupils in an organised form. This makes their learning more effective.

5. ***Knowledge of Problems.*** Through the medium of lesson planning, the teacher thinks out the problems and difficulties relating to the lesson and how to solve them.

6. ***Dreaming Objectives.*** For teaching a subject, lesson planning is necessary, to define the objectives, offer a norm for organising and evacuating the subject-matter.

7. ***Development of Mental Power.*** The lesson plan helps in developing reasoning, decision making, imagination in the pupils.

8. ***To Establish Relationship between Teaching and Learning.*** Through lesson planning practical relationship can be established between teaching and learning. In education, close relationship. between teaching and learning is very necessary. So, for this purpose lesson planning is helpful.

9. ***Utility of Individual Differences.*** Keeping individual differences of the pupils in mind, he can prepare various kinds of lesson plans.

10. ***For Reinforcement.*** Through lesson planning the teacher decides pupils activities and the situations for using devices for reinforcement.

11. ***To Control Indiscipline.*** At times, the cause of indiscipline in the class, is lack of preparation on the part of the teacher. So planning of lesson is important and essential for handling such problems.

12. ***For Interesting Teaching.*** To make lesson interesting, clear and simple, it is necessary to select in advance, the relevant methods, devices and strategies. To achieve this aim, the teacher must prepare the lesson plan before hand.

13. ***New Knowledge on the Basis of Previous Knowledge.*** In the lesson plan, new knowledge is given on the basic of previous knowledge. This accounts for newness and simplification of the lesson. All activities, of class level and suitable to syllabus, are selected in advance. This creates interest of the students in the lesson.

14. ***To Provide Outline.*** In teacher training, the lesson plan presents the outline of the class activities.

Thus we see, how important and necessary is lesson planning in modern age. On psychological grounds too, lesson plan offers moral strength to the teacher. So, before going to the class the teacher should prepare the lesson plan.

PREPARATION OF LESSON PLAN

Educational world and teacher under training are highly indebted to the great educationist Herbart, a leading exponent of psychological tendencies in education for his Five Harbartian Steps. According to him teaching is not a right process. It depends more on the resourcefullness and way of handling of the subject-matter by the teacher of Social Studies than the application of the old orthodox and conservative educational, principles or doctrines. But a few general principles for preparing it lesson-plan can briefly be laid down for the guidance of the young under-trainees.

(a) A lesson plan should always be drawn psychologically.

(b) It should be arranged properly, sub-headings should be mentioned briefly and specifically.

(c) While drawing a lesson plan in social studies or social sciences a teacher should take advantage of the different maxims of teaching like from known to unknown, from particular to general, from concrete to abstract and from immediate to the remote or from the present to the past, etc.

(d) A lesson of history plan should have the accurate consideration of time and space whereas a lesson of geography should have, accurate consideration of cause and effect. If stories whether of history or geography are selected at junior stage, they should be arranged in chronological order.

(e) It is always advisable to divide the lesson plan into different units. Each unit should be given the up-to-date treatment it deserves.

These steps start after we have fulfilled the formal blackboard entries like, class, subject, topic, time, period and average age of the students.

1. General Aims. General aims of various branches of Social Studies more or less remain the same. Following may be stated briefly as the general aims of social studies.

(a) To let the students understand the evolutionary process of growth of human society.

(b) Enrichment and development of the lives of the pupils in their natural and social environment.

(c) To develop the power of imagination, reasoning and judgement through the teaching of Social Studies.

(d) To make the students intelligent, patriotic and also to develop a cosmopolitan outlook in the students *i.e.* socialisation of students and promotion of international understanding.

(e) To prepare the students for the future. To make them familiar with the present as the outcome of the past. It means let them understand the experiences of the race.

(f) Training in desirable pattern of conduct.

(g) Formation of habits and skills.

It is not necessary that all the aims stated above can be achieved in a lesson but the teacher has to strived realise as many aims as is possible in various lessons.

2. Specific Aim. The specific aim is concerned with the topic of the lesson. It should be written quite particularly and clearly. It should give the idea of what the teacher actually wants to achieve with the teaching of that topic. The specific aim, it should be borne in mind, should never be long and complex.

3. Material Aid. Material aid is needed to create an effective atmosphere in the teaching of the lesson. But it is not necessarily essential to produce it in every lesson. The following qualities of a good material aid should be borne in mind while selecting them.

(i) It should be relevant to the topic under discussion.

(ii) It should be produced at the proper time when the lesson is going on.

(iii) It should not be too costly.

(iv) It is better to draw diagrams, sketch, maps on the blackboard and in the presence of the students.

(v) The teacher should make a proper arrangement for the production of the material. If pictures and models are used, they should not be removed immediately. Let the students should form their impression in their mind.

4. Previous Knowledge Assumed. A teacher should be very careful in his assumption of the previous knowledge. The introduction of the new lesson will depend on a correct assumption of the previous knowledge. It can make the effectiveness of the introductory stage.

5. Introduction. This is indeed the beginning of the lesson. This is a stage with its unique importance. Well begun is half done holds true in this case. Following are the aims of introductory stage.

Aims

(a) To create an effective atmosphere for the teaching of the new lesson.

(b) To test the previous knowledge.

(c) To create preparedness in the students for the reception of the new knowledge.

What should be the Qualities of a Good Introduction?

(a) It should be neither too long nor too short, four to six questions are sufficient.

(b) All the questions should have psychological arrangements.

(c) It should be based upon the previous knowledge assumed.

(d) It should not be vague and indefinite.

At the stage of introduction, the teacher should have the performance like a juggler. Juggler seldom starts the demonstration of his feats unless he has been able to catch the attention of his spectators. A teacher should consider his introductory task successful, only when he has been able to develop curiosity among the pupils at this stage. The success of the lesson to a large extent depends upon the successful performance of the introductory stage.

6. Statement of Aim. After the introductory work is over, the teacher should give the statement of aim. The statement of the aim should have the following questions.

(a) It should be explained strictly the aim of that particular lesson. It should not be vague and indefinite.

(b) It should be emphasised the utility of that particular lesson in the present day.

(c) It should be brief and well wooded. It is not sufficient to state that "To-day, we shall read about Ashoka but a good

form of it would be To-day we shall try to be familiar with the significant reign of Ashoka whose integrity, piety and devotion to duty has affected the modern society of ours."

7. Presentation. This is a stage for the transmission of the new knowledge to the students. The stage of presentation does not present such a great difficulty in the language lesson as in case of Social sciences such as geography, economics, civics and history, The following points should be taken into consideration at the stage of presentation of Social Studies lesson..

(a) It should be divided into units. It is always better to divide the stage of presentation into two or three units.

(b) The presentation is to be divided into two parts *i.e.*, Matter and Method plus expected answers from the students.

(c) The subject-matter should be arranged in a chronological manner.

(d) A few questions should be put to the students to test and develop the time-sense of the students.

(e) Use of regressive method should be made whenever and wherever it is possible.

(f) It is always better to develop the presentation in the form of questions in order to secure more cooperation of the class.

(g) There should be psychological link between questions. Where psychological link is not possible because of dissimilarity between the nature of two questions, they should be connected with the intervening statement of the teacher. One question should lead the other.

(h) The presents should be linked with the past whenever and wherever it is possible.

(i) The following types of question should be avoided

(i) Questions of complex nature.

(ii) Questions not properly wonded.

(*iii*) Suggestive questions.

(*iv*) Questions have answers in the form of 'yes.' or 'no'.

(*v*) Abstract questions.

(*j*) Questions should be thought provoking.

(*k*) The form of question should not be changed very often otherwise the students can get confused. If need be, the form or question can be changed when the teacher is satisfied that a slight change in the form may help in eliciting quick response from the students.

(*l*) Whenever and wherever it is possible, generalisation should be drawn.

(*m*) Lastly, presentation should suit the mental level and academic standard of the students for whom it is meant.

8. Black-Board Summary. It is an index of teacher's work with the class. Following points may be specified here for guidance in this respect.

(i) Preferably, Black-Board summary should be developed along with the lesson.

(ii) Complex sentences should be avoided. It should merely be develop in main and significant points.

(iii) It should be a summary of the lesson and not supplementary to it.

(iv) Black-Board handwriting should be neat, bold and uniform.

9. Home-Task. A teacher should give a proper thought before it is assigned to the class. Before he assigns home-task he should bear the following points in mind.

(*i*) Its main objective is to use properly the leisure time of the students.

(*ii*) It should be given in coordination with other subject teacher.

(iii) It should have variety *i.e.* long answer types, short answer types, objective types, filling the gap, preparation of diagram, maps, or if possible, making of models.

ADVANTAGES OF LESSON PLANNING

1. Planning of a lesson helps the teacher to organise his teaching thoroughly.
2. The teacher of Social Studies is clear about the knowledge already gained by the students and what more he is expected to teach them.
3. With lesson planning sequence of the information supplied about various facts is maintained.
4. By doing so teaching becomes more clear and effective.
5. The information about the topic is imparted to the students step by step and not in a haphazard manner.
6. Lesson plan helps to link the old knowledge with new one.
7. The sectional/partial recapitulation is very necessary if the lesson in Social Studies, is long. This step is for reinforcement of knowledge.

HERBARTIAN APPROACH OF LESSON-PLAN

Taking the five steps of Herbart, as the base, the following steps of the lesson plan can be set. Following these, pupil-teachers can write their own lesson plans.

(i) ***Subject, Topic, Class, Section, Period and Date.*** The lesson plan is prepared, after deciding these points. According to the subject, choice is made of the topic, and sub-topic.

(ii) ***General Objectives.*** His necessary to set some general aims to back the lesson. The success of teaching depends upon achieving these objectives. Evaluation of teachers teaching is also done with reference to these general objectives.

(iii) ***Teaching Aids.*** The teacher has to decide about the aids to be used in the lesson *e.g.* the use of the black-board, model/chart, radio/tape recorder projector, television etc.

(iv) ***Previous Knowledge.*** In teaching, it is necessary to think about previous knowledge. So as to teach new knowledge. For teaching new knowledge, the previous knowledge acts as its base.

(v) ***Specific Aim.*** This objective is based on the central theme of the lesson. It is fixed up on the basis of the subject-matter.

(vi) ***Introduction.*** It is based on the previous knowledge of the pupils. The new lesson is reached through the medium of the introduction. This step, in the lesson plan is considered as very important. For introduction, questions are asked on previous knowledge, to link with the new topic: For this he puts three to four questions, so that the proposed topic may be linked with the previous knowledge.

(vii) ***Statement of Aim.*** The teacher, relating to the topic, announces that we shall study this topic today.

(viii) ***Presentation.*** The practical part of the lesson begins with presentation. At this stage, the teacher must motivate the pupils. Questions are put in this step for the progress of the lesson.

(ix) ***Recapitulation.*** To revise the lesson taught is called recapitulation. This enables one to know, about the success of the lesson. With getting correct answers of recapitulatory questions the success of teaching can be guessed. If the lesson is divided into units, then after every unit, revision should be there.

(x) ***Home-Work.*** The importance of home-work, in teaching is second to none. So, the hometask must be given. Different types of questions can be given in home-task step.

(xi) ***Clarification.*** On getting no reply to these developmental questions, the teacher himself offers explanation so that there remains no doubt or conflict in the minds of the pupils.

(xii) ***Black-Board Summary.*** The teacher writes the teaching points on the black-board. The black-board happens to be his friend. Without this, the teacher cannot be successful. The black-board summary should be written simultaneously or after the teacher's narration is over.

MERITS OF HERBARTIAN APPROACH

1. It is based upon psychological principles.
2. Its nature is, well organised and well controlled.
3. It can be used for all subjects.
4. Its use simplifies lesson planning task.
5. It is powerful for bringing unconscious thoughts to conscious mind.
6. It uses Inductive and Deductive methods.
7. It teaches how to use the newly learned knowledge in new situations.
8. It is based upon previously learned knowledge.
9. The pupils are active and get opportunities to think originally.
10. All knowledge is gained in a coordinated manner.

DEMERITS OF HARBARTIAN APPROACH

1. There is more emphasis on presentation.
2. Teacher's freedom is limited.
3. With this approach only knowledge lessons can be taught effectively, whereas for skill and appreciation lessons it is not suitable.
4. The lesson plan is less flexible.
5. Less attention is paid to pupils interests and aptitudes.

6. Teaching objectives and learning conditions are not kept under considerations.
7. Teaching comes to memory level.
8. In the lesson plan the specification of teaching objectives is not done.

CHARACTERISTICS OF GOOD LESSON PLAN

The lesson plan should have the following characteristics:

- It should be written.
- It should be related to previous knowledge.
- It should explicitly mention general and specific objectives.
- Adequate care should be there in the selection of subject-matter.
- There should be clear indication of activities involved in the lesson.
- It should be based upon good teaching methods.
- It should be suitable to the child's interests, tendencies, capabilities and aptitudes.
- Should be based on individual differences.
- Should be related to life situations.
- It should make use of examples and aids so that the lesson becomes simple, interesting and easily comprehensible.
- It should give expected space to every point.
- It should have provision for the pupils to choose activities and scope for guidance.
- It should give room for assignments.
- Should mention home task.
- It should have place for criticism of the lesson.
- Should be divided into units.
- It should be neat and clean, beautiful.

The lesson plan is a servant and not the master of the teacher. He should be active throughout the lesson. Having decided the teachers and pupils activities, the plan should be flexible as to permit the teacher to make change as per conditions to cope up and to leave no scope for going astray, so that the majority of pupils may take full interest in the lesson.

LESSON PLAN

Pupil Teachers Name	:	--			
Roll No.	:	----------------	Date	:	------------
Class	:	VIII	Duration	:	------------
Average Age	:	12+Years	Topic	:	Mineral-Resources
Subject	:	Social Studies			

Behavioural Objectives

After studying this lesson the student:

1. Names the main minerals founding in India,
2. States the uses of Iron,
3. Shows the main centres of iron ore
4. Recalls the uses and main centres of coal production,
5. States the uses of mica,
6. Names the main centres of mica production,
7. Mentions the uses of maganese,
8. States the main production centres of maganese,
9. States the main production centres of bauxite,
10. Recalls the uses and production centres of mineral oil,
11. Names the distress based on minerals.

Teaching Aids

1. Specimen of mineral.
2. Map of India—Mineral distribution.

Previous Knowledge

Students have seen ornaments made of silver and gold. They have also seen articles made of iron. They are also familiar with the word mineral. Introduction (Testing of Previous knowledge)

(Showing Ornaments)

1. What is this?
2. What is it made of?
3. What fuel is used in village homes?
4. Where-from do we get gold, iron and coal ?

(PROBLEM QUESTION)

Statement of Aim

Students, to-day we will study minerals and the industries based on them.

Presentation of Lesson

Lesson will be presented through question-answer and lecture method.

Content	*Pupil-teacher Activities*	*Student Activities*	*Black-board work*
Minerls	Name the important minerals found in India	Answers	Iron, coal, Mica, Manganese, bauxite and mineral
Iron	What are the main uses of iron?	Answers	Iron is used to make machines, Railway engine, Rail Motor car, weight and masurer etc.
	Name the industries based on iron.	Answers	Iron and steel, machine etc.
	What are the main centres of iron production?	Unsatis-factory Answer	

Pupil-Teacher Statement. Mayur Bhanj in Orissa, Distt. Bhuwan in Bihar; other centres are located in Madhya Pradesh, Andhra Pradesh, Karnatak and Maharashtra.

Coal	What are the main uses of Coal?	Answers	Coal is the main source of energy. It is used to run factories Railways and ships.
	What are the main centres of coal production.	Answers	Jhariya in Bihar and Raniganj. in West Bengal.
	What are the other important States in the field of Coal production.	Unsatisfactory Answer	

Pupil-Teacher Statement. Mica is used in electric appliances for the following reasons:

1. Mica is a bad conductor of heat.
2. Mica does not melt even at hundred of celcius temperature.

Narrates the position of India in the field of Mica production.	Listens Attentively	India occupies an important place in the world in the field of Mica production. Nearly 3/4 of production is exported. Hazari Bagh in Bihar is the main area in the production of Mica.
Name the other States producing Mica.	Answers	

Pupil-Teacher Statement. Other important fields are Distt. Nellore in Andhra Pradesh, Bhilwara in Rajasthan. Some Mica is also found in Madhya Pradesh, Tamil Nadu and Kashmir.

Manganese	What are the uses of maganese?	Answers	Manganese is mainly used for making steel and painting the glass.
	What are the main centres of Manganese production?	Unsatisfactory Answer	

Pupil-Teacher's Statement. Main centres of Maganese mining are found Palaghat in Madhya Pradesh, Nagpur in Maharashtra, Karnatka, Bihar, Andhra Pradesh and Rajasthan.

Bauxite	State the uses of Bauxite.	States	Bauxite is to make a aluminium. It is used in making aeroplanes and electric wires.
	What are the main mining centres?	Unsatis factory Answers.	

Pupil-Teacher's Statement. South Bihar, Orissa, Karnataka, Maharashtra, Tamil Nadu are known for mining Bauxite.

Mineral oil	What are the main uses of mineral oil?	Answers	Mineral oil is an important source of fuel. It is used in buses, motor cars, aeroplanes etc.
	What are the main centres of mineral oil production.	Answers	Digboi in Assam, Ankleshwar in Gujarat and Bombay High.

Pupil-Teacher's Statement. Staudents, you are right. But recent researches surveys have shown the possibilities of getting mineral oil in Tarai region.

Recepitulation

1. Write one use of each of the following mineral:
   - *(i)* Iron ....
   - *(ii)* Coal ....
   - *(iii)* Mica ....
   - *(iv)* Maganese ....
   - *(v)* Bauxite ....
   - *(vi)* Mineral oil ....
2. Name four industries based on minerals.
3. Carefully study the map of India-minerals and answer the following questions:

(i) States very rich in minerals.

(ii) States which have least mineral wealth.

(iii) States which have no mineral wealth.

Home-Task

Complete the table given below:

Name of the Mineral	*Production centres*	*use*	*Industry*
Iron			
Coal			
Mica			
Maganese			
Bauxite			

LESSON PLAN NO. 1
(HISTORY)

Roll No of the pupil-teacher	. . . .
Class	IX
Subject	Social Studies
Average Age of the Pupil	14 years
Duration	40 minutes
Topic	First War of Indian Independence
Date	. . . .

Illustrative Material with the Teacher

(1) Class-room apparatus—chalk, duster, black-board.

(2) Map of India.

(3) Chart showing the army generals of the first war of Indian independence.

AIMS OF THE LESSON

General Aims

(1) To develop mental growth of students.

(2) To develop love and pride for the nation.

(3) To develop ability to express their thoughts freely and effectively.

Specific Aims

To acquaint students with the first war of Indian independence.

Students Previous Knowledge

Students already known about struggle for freedom carried out mainly on two occasions.

Introduction Students Knowledge of Testing

The following questions will be put to students to test their previous knowledge.

(1) What do you understand by the term freedom?

(2) When did India achieve freedom?

(3) How many times did India carry out struggle to win freedom?

Announcement of the Aim

Today, we shall study about the first war of Indian independence.

Presentation

Matter	*Method*	*B. B. Summary*
1	*2*	*3*
In 1857, the Indian army and the people of India revolted against British power. This was the first attempt to get freedom from British imperialism. Historians are divided amongst themselves on	When did the Indian army revolt against the British power?	In 1857
this issue. According to some it was only the sepoy revolt and still others consider it as an attempt	What are the views of different	Some called it a revolt, others an attempt to

Contd.

1	*2*	*3*
to get back the lost freedom while others view it as the national struggle for freedom. Whether the revolt was pre-planned or not, or people took part in it as one nation or not some historians believe this revolt suddenly occurred when soldiers were compelled to use the cartridges having cow's fat. Others take it as a pre-planned development.	historians about the first war of independence?	get back the lost freedom for trade.
The people took part in it, to get freedom for India by bringing an end to the British rule. Common people — Hindus and Muslims participated alike in this struggle Kr. Singh, Rani Laxmi Bai, Tanya Tope, Mughal Emperor Bahadurshah, Nanasahib the leaders of this struggle and sacrificed their lives to get freedom for their country.	Who are the leaders of this struggle?	Rani of Jhansi Laxmi Bai, Mughal Emperor Bahadurshah, Tantya Tope
Causes. There were following causes of the first war of independence:		
(i) Political Causes. From Lord Wellesly to Lord Dulhousie almost all Governor Generals followed the policy of extending the British empire by fair or fowl means. The Maratha states were liquidated. Sind and Pubjab were forcibly annexed. The Nawab of the Sind was deprived of his Nawabship,		

Contd.

1	2	3
Satara, Jhansi, Nagpur, Udaipur were merged, in the English kingdom Since their rulers were issueless. The pension of the Peshwa was discontinued. Owing to merger of states, many soldiers were rendered unemployed. Bahadur Shah lost his throne, this angered the Muslims.	Which states were merged in the British kingdom?	Satara, Jhansi, Nagpur, Udaipur, Sind, Punjab
(ii) Military Causes. Indians were in big number in the English army. According to the new rule, they could be sent to all places, across the seas. This created discontent since it was against their religions. Again, they were given cartridges having pig and cow's fat. Because of the merger of the Indian states, their armies were disbanded. Those unemployed soldiers became bitter enemies of the Britishers.	Why were the Indian soldiers discontented	Because of interference in their religion.
(iii) Religious Reasons. The clergies were extensively propagating Christianity among Indian people. They enticed the simple folk, by giving money and converting them to Christianity. In addition the people were displeased because of the rules for bringing about social reforms. The Britishers committed a blunder by changing law of inheritance. People thought that	How were the Britishers preaching their religion?	Through conversions and use of money.

Contd.

(ii) Objective. Critical thinking

Himalayas which have been guarding the boundaries of India since centuries are no more invincible due to the fact that:

(a) Many passes have been discovered in Himalayas.

(b) Superior type of war material has been developed.

(c) Nations across the Himalayas have become too hostile and aggressive.

(d) The climate of the mountain regions has changed.

(e) Techniques of blasting the mountains have been much improved.

(iii) Objective. Critical thinking.

Government of Bihar wants to establish a big iron and steel plant in the country. Which of the following factors may be ignored in selecting a place for this plant?

(a) Cheap labour is available.

(b) Political leaders are not interested.

(c) Electric power is available.

(d) Necessary raw material is available.

(iv) Objective. Knowledge

Which one of the following is the best safeguard for fundamental rights?

(a) Strong opposition in the legislature

(b) Removal of provision for emergency

(c) Inexpensive and speedy justice

(c) Removal of limitations placed on them

(v) Objective. Understanding

Tick off the correct answer:

The chief characteristic of climate in Mediterranean lands is-

(a) Hot wet summers and cold dry winters

(b) Hot dry summers and cold wet winters

(c) Hot dry summers and warm dry winters

(vi) *Objective.* Understanding (Comparison)

The difference between the functioning of the League of Nations and the UNO becomes most evident from the comparison of the two with regard to:

(a) Great Power Balance

(b) Disarmament

(c) Collective Security

(d) Forum for Dialogue on International Disputes

(e) Political status quo.

(vii) *Objective.* Critical thinking (Location of the sources of information)

Which part of the Indian constitution will you look for to ascertain how the provision of freedom to follow one's religion has been laid down?

(a) Preamble

(b) Citizenship

(c) Fundamental Rights

(d) Directive Principles

(e) Parliament Procedures

Suggestions on the Construction of Multiple Choice Items

1. *Four to Five Items.* The number of items must not be less than four as this will minimise guessing. More than five, however, will tax the child in reading.

2. *No Non-parallel or Non-homogeneous Options.* In one and the same test, non-parallel or non-homogeneous options must not be given as in the following:

The Prime Minister of India.

(i) is named Atal Behari Bajpai

(ii) is elected by the people

(iii) is appointed for six years

3. *Different Positions of Correct Choice.* The correct choice must occupy the different answer positions in the different items.

4. *Concise Items.* The items should not be weighed with unnecessary material. They must be as concise as possible.

5. *Single Correct Answer.* There should be only one correct answer.

6. *Same Length of Answers.* Right and wrong answers must be roughly of the same length otherwise the mere physical appearance of the questions will afford clues to the child.

(2) True or False or Yes-No. Here a few statements are given of which some are true and some are false. The pupil is required to put 'T' or 'V' against true and 'F' or 'No' against false statements for example:

(i) Vice-President, as a matter of course, becomes the President of India for a limited duration only. (Understanding)

(ii) A person holding the office of the governor can be a candidate for election as the President of India. (Understanding)

(iii) Krishna was born before Christ. (Knowledge).

(iv) The Prime Minister always works on the advice of the cabinet. (Knowledge)

(3) Completion Type. In completion type tests questions asked involve the filling in of a proper name, date, significant facts, etc. Such type of questions elicit knowledge of facts.

Examples

(i) A person holding the office of the....is eligible to become the President of India.

(Collector, Governor, Commissioner, Major-General, Army contractor) *(ii)* The......is elected by both the houses of Parliament.

(President, Vice- President, Prime Minister, Speaker, Chief Justice of India).

(iii) The cabinet may not approve proposals for embodying the policies of the government (legislation, budget, senior promotion, judicial punishment, enquiry committees).

(iv) The office of Prime Minister of India is (elective, hereditary, nominative).

(4) Sequence Tests. In sequence test, some haphazard items are given which are to be arranged in chronological order:

Examples

1. Arrange the following in sequence:

   Cripps Mission

   Third Battle of Panipat

   Minto-Morley Reforms

   The Tragedy of Jallianwala Bagh

   First War of Indian Independence

   Battle of Plassey

   Salt March

2. Rearrange the following industries of the Himalayan region in order of their importance:

   (a) Forest ( )

   (b) Tourism ( )

   (c) Fishing ( )

   (d) Agriculture ( )

   (e) Mining ( )

(5) Matching Test. In matching test, two lists of items are given without any order or arrangement. The pupils have to match items from one list with appropriate, items of the other list. The test seeks to test the understanding of facts:

Example 1. Match the following geographical areas and the products.

1. Patagonia	1. Ouebracco logs
2. Mendoza	2. Frozen Meat
3. Uspallata	3. Sugar refineries
4. Buenos Aires	4. Petroleum
5. Theoman	5. Mountain Pass
6. River Paraguay	6. Wine
	7. Grasslands
	8. Lake

Example 2. Match the types of towns with names:

1. Confluence town	1. Sindri
2. Port town	2. Delhi
3. Religious town	3. Hazaribagh
4. Health resort	4. Banaras
5. Industrial town	5. Ranchi
6. Mining town	6. Allahabad
7. Capital town	7. Sarnath
	8. Raniganj
	9. Kolkata

(6) Classification Tests. This type of test is used for ability to classify facts.

Example 1. Underline the odd name out:

(i) Guru Nanak, Christ, Hazrat Mohammad, Arya Bhata.

(ii) Akbar, Chandragupta Vikramaditya, Jahangir, Chingiz Khan.

Example 2. Given below is the list of agricultural produce, mineral resources and manufactured goods of seven countries—Myanmar, India, Japan, Malaysia, Pakistan, United Kingdom and United States.

1. Rice, 2. Wheat, 3. Oilseeds and vegetable oils, 4. Tea, 5. Rubber, 6. Hides and Skins, 7. Coal, 8. Iron ore, 9. Manganese ore, 10. Mica, 11. Mineral oil, 12. Uranium, 13. Cotton Textiles, 14. Linen or Jute Textiles, 15. Metal goods, 16. Machines and tools.

Sort out and classify the above items in the appropriate columns in the following table:

Name of the country	*Item nos. which are not enough for the country to meet its own requirements*	*Item nos. which are just enough for the country to meet its own requirements*	*Item nos. which the country has enough to spare for others*
Myanmar			
India			
Japan			
Malaysia			
Pakistan			
United Kingdom			
United States			

(7) Relationship Test. Relationship between the two things is asked in this test, intended to test understanding:

Examples:

1. For each event given below, mention place and year with which you associate it.

Event	Place	Year
Birth of M.K.Gandhi	......	......
Foundation of League of Nations	.....	......

2. Suppose were a high caste Brahmin lady living through the Arundhati following period of Indian history.

   (a) Later Vedic Age (LY.A.)

   (b) Gupta Age (G.A.)

   (c) Medieval Age (MA.)

   (d) Post Independence India (P.I.I.)

Read the statements given below in a tabular form describing some aspects of her life. Each statement relates to the conditions of social life prevailing in all the four periods of Indian history. Put a tick mark (✓) within the brackets under the period wherein the condition is true.

Statement	LVA	GA	MA	PII
(i) She could move about in the street without purdah.	( )	( )	( )	( )
(ii) She could get high education.	( )	( )	( )	( )
(iii) She could have equal political rights as men.	( )	( )	( )	( )
(iv) She could marry outside her caste.	( )	( )	( )	( )
(v) She could divorce her husband.	( )	( )	( )	( )

EVALUATION PROGRAMME IN SOCIAL STUDIES

A complete evaluation programme in Social Studies should include the following tests.

1. Essay-type test
2. Objective-type test
3. Assignments
4. Cumulative Records
5. Oral test

1. Eassy-type Test. These tests are designed to judge the pupil's knowledge in Social Studies as expresson in a limited number of questions of a discussion type. In case of a vast subject like Social Studies, these tests occupy an important place. They can test a wide range of abilities, including critical thinking, interpretation, reasoning and judgement. A student can discuss a topic fully or a problem in detail in all its relationships. Essay-type tests are also used to measure other objectives such as attitudes towards certain social, political or economic phenomena. These tests allow the students a greater freedom of expression and response. Subjectivity in marking answer books does come when some of the examiners are too liberal and others too strict. This is only reason why objective-type tests are recommended to supplement essay-type tests on all occasions. To make these tests more effective questions on the construction of graphs, filling up of maps, preparation of charts and time-lines. etc, should also form an important part of evaluation through essay-type tests.

2. Objective-type Tests. The objective-type tests form the latest technique in testing. There are two general types of objective tests in common use:

(a) The standardized tests

(b) Teacher-mode tests

(A) ***The Standardized Tests.*** The standardized of objective tests in social studies is the work of experts who have established their validity and reliability, fixed definite and uniform procedures for administering them and provided keys for scoring.

Standardized tests are of four types:

(i) Achievement test is desingned to measure the attainment in Social Studies. This test is more widely used in school than any other kind.

(ii) The diagnostic test is designed to measure a large Number of abilities, interests and performances including techniques, skills and forms of information which are essential for success in the subject as a whole.

(iii) The intelligent test is designed to measure mental ability—the ability to learn and to adapt on-self to new situations. An intelligence test can be used both for group testing and individual testing. But the results of individual tests are more reliable and accurate than those of group tests.

(iv) The aptitude and personality test is intended to measure the traits of temperaments and character. Both tests are usually designed in the form of inventories and rating scale and therefore, their approach is more qualitative than quantitative.

Standardized tests are therefore, extremely helpful in finding out a child's good points and weak points by comparing him with other pupils of the same age. In India, the majority of our schools cannot make use of these tests because of their expenses and non-availability.

(B) ***Teacher-mode Tests.*** These tests are constructed by the teacher himself, according to his philosophy of education. These are of various kinds:

(i) *Recall or Question and Answer Form.* The simplest form of new type test in Social Studies is the recall. It consists in asking a direct question, having one definite answer. It is suited to the recall of names and dates, such as,

(a) Who was the founder of Buddhism?

(b) In what year was the First Battle of Panipat fought?

(ii) *Completion Form.* It is that type of test in which a single word or a phrase answer is required in one or two parts of a sentence to complete it, such as:

1. The first battle of Panipat was fought between ...... and
2. The Britishers first came to India as traders and formed in 1600 the company. Their trade rivals in India were ......

(c) *True False or Yes-No Form.* This is the best known of the objective type tests. In this test a statement is made and the student is asked to say whether the statement is true or false, such as:

1. Razia Begum was a famous Mughal queen. Yes/No

   Was Razia Begum a famous Mughal queen? Yes/No

2. Godawari is the most important river in China. Yes/No

   Is Godawari the most important river in China? Yes/No

(d) *Multiple Choice Form.* In this case a statement is made and several choices are given, only one of which makes the statement true. The student is required to underline the correct choice, such as:

(i) The governor of a state in India is

(1) appointed by the Chief Minister of the state concerned.

(2) elected by the members of the Legislative Assembly.

(3) nominated by the Prime Minister of India.

(4) appointed by the President of Indian Union.

(ii) The capital of Bengal is Patna, Kolkata, Bikaner, Allahabad.

(e) *Matching Form.* In this case two sets of statements, one consisting of causes and the other results, are given. The pupil is required to connect each result with the proper cause, such as:

Place the number of each item in column I, beside the correct name in Column II.

Column I	Column II
1. Father of the Nation	Rajinder Parshad
2. President of Indian Republic	Krishna
3. A River in the Deccan	Mahatma Gandhi
4. Author of the Gitanjali	Kabir
5. A great reformer of India	Tagore
6. Author of Discovery of India	Jawahar lal Nehru

(f) *Time-Sequence Form.* This type of question contains a list of items which a student is required to re-arrange on the basis of chronology, such as, indicate the chronological order of the events in the following group by numbering the items 1,2,3,4 and 5.

- Fahien's visit to India
- Alexander's invasion of India
- First battle of Panipat
- Birth of Akbar
- Taj Mahal

3. Testing through Assignments. Assignment is a supplement to class-room teaching. But each assignment should be very carefully prepared by the teacher. References to study, books, journals, magazines, papers, etc. to be consulted and a list of such books should be given along with the assignments. Weekly assignments for school students are better than monthly or daily assignments. Time-limit should be given for each assignment and then the assignments should be collected for evaluation. Assignments in Social Studies are very useful for the revision of a topic or unit learnt in the class. These may also be in the form of preparing a chart, model or writing a detailed account of some current or historical event at home. An assignment challenges the intellectual and thinking powers of school children. If the assignments are regularly and properly checked and evaluated by the teacher, he will discover many traits of attainments of his students.

4. Testing through Cumulative Records. As we have already noted, emphasis on only one annual examination must disappear. The ability and proficiency of a child should not be judged according to the results of the final examination alone but on the progress as shown in the school records. This objective is being achieved in educationally advanced countries by the introduction of Cumulative Record Cards. A cumulative record for every pupil is maintained in each school. It indicates the work done by the pupil in the school from day to day, from month to month, from term to term and year to year. It contains attainments in different intellectual pursuits. In fact, a cumulative record gives a comprehensive picture of the all-round development of the child's personality.

Such a record should be maintained by the class teacher from year to year. It should follow the student as he is promoted from class to class or as he moves from one school to another.

ESSAY-TYPE EXAMINATION IN SOCIAL STUDIES

Much has been said against the present day system of examination. Teachers, parents and students have been often seen complaining against the essay-type of examination as something useless and something which encourages cram work.

Whereas the present system of examination is generally unsatisfactory it is more so in the case of Social Studies. It does not demand an ability to think or to correlate facts but only to reproduce what the students have learnt from the text or help books.

An examination has an educative value. It is not only a means of training that the students have learnt but also instructs them as it is a sort of revision. It gives them excellent opportunity to apply the knowledge gained from the lesson and the book. In an ideal extenuation, the teacher corrects the answer and guides the students in the management and correlation of facts. But in reality the examination today is not what it ought to have been and a good deal of revision and improvement is necessary.

The following main objections have been raised against the present day Essay-type examination in Social Studies:

I. **It is a Poor and Inadequate Means of Testing Knowledge of Social Studies.** The essay type of examination is a poor means of testing the knowledge of various Social sciences which constitute Social Studies. The courses of Social Studies for the different classes are so wide that five or six essay type questions cannot test whether a student knows all about the prescribed course of a particular class.

II. **Involves a Lot of Guess Work.** What the students do is to pick and select some most important questions from the examination point of view and learn their answers thoughly well. Thus, this system encourages cram work and those who can cram well can score well. Intelligent students who are poor at cramming lag behind in respect of marks obtained in such type of examination.

III. **It Involves Language Difficulties.** The language difficulty is another serious defect in this type of examination. Some students are good, it languages and have good capacity to express but poor knowledge of Social Studies, may beat those who have poor command of language. Speed and good hand-writing are also factors which count in scoring good marks, in this subject.

Those who decry this type of examination offer a substitute called the new type of tests called Objective-type of tests.

Under mentioned are some of the objective type of tests for Social Studies:

1. True/False Tests. In this type of test a series of statements are given and students are asked, to put a 'yes' or no' sign against each of statements. In this the students knowledge of facts and their judgement are tested. As for example, the students may be called upon to put 'yes' or 'no' or 'True' or 'False' against each of the following statements.

Examples. Which of these statements is 'correct' or 'True' and which one 'False' ?

(a) Queen Elizabeth was a great queen of Great Britain.

(b) Akbar was the father of Aurangzeb.

(c) Cotton is grown in Tamil Nadu.

(d) Various types of minerals are found in Kerala state.

2. The Multiple Choice Tests. In this test the student has to pick out a true statement from several alternative statements. This test can be used to test the students knowledge of facts, dates, judgement, etc. It is an improvement on the true/false test.

(i) Testing of Knowledge Facts:

(a) Akbar was a contemporary of Queen Elizabeth or King Charles or King James.

(b) Tantiatope was a king, general, a minister.

(c) Tea is grown in the Punjab, Assam, Bihar.

(d) Gujarat state is famous for the growth of jute, cotton, sugarcane.

(ii) Testing of Dates:

(a) Akabar was born in 1625, 1525, 1725.

(b) Third battle of Panipat was faught in 1756, 1666, 1761.

(c) India won freedom in 1947, 1957, 1937.

(iii) Testing of Judgement. Which of the three sentence is nearest the truth in your opinion.

(a) Indian First War of Independence in 1857 was an ordinary revolt.

(b) It was a Great War of Independence.

(c) It was just a riot.

(iv) Completion Test. In this test, the students are given some incomplete sentences and are required to complete them.

(a) Jute is grown in the state of

(b) In India there are religions like Hinduism,

(c) Second Battle of Panipat was fought in

(d) Theory of rent was defined by

(v) The Matching Test. In this test the students are given two parallel lists of words and date or states and production and they have to match one for the first to last.

I	II
(a) Death of Aurangzeb	1751
(b) Vasco da Gama	Chinese traveller
(c) Second Battle of Panipat	1556
(d) Heun Tsang	An explorer
(e) Assam	minerals
(f) Bihar	tea

(vi) Time Sequence Test. In this test, students are required to show the sequence of events. They are given a list of facts and have to arrange their in correct time sequence.

Arrange the following facts in chronological order.

(i) Death of Babar.

(ii) Battle of Thanesar.

(iii) Accession of Harsh Vardhan.

(iv) Battle of Kalinga.

(v) Reign of Altmash.

Merits

These objective type tests have certain distinct advantages over the old essay type of examination. The main merits of these tests are as follows:

(1) Knowledge of a large number of facts can be tested in a short period of time.

(2) The students do not have to write much and eliminate the difficulty or hindrance of the language.

(3) They discourage cram work.

(4) They enable us to test not only knowledge but time-sense, casual relationship, judgement and cause and effective relationship also.

(5) The making of scripts is easy in these tests.

(6) Scores of questions can be set to cover the entire syllabus.

Demerits

They have certain demerits which are given below:

1. Question-papers of these tests are almost as lengthy as the answer paper. One question-paper sometime consists of 5 to 6 pages.

2. Preparation of a test-paper requires a great deal of experience and skill on the part of paper setter and all teachers are not sufficiently experienced and skilful to handle these tests. Test paper involving judgement are all the more difficult to construct and later on to evaluate it.

3. Whereas essay-type tests encourage cram work. These objective type tests encourage guess work, this is true in case of yes/no, true/false question papers. If a student writes 'yes' or 'no' at random against each sentence, some of them may come out correct. The same can happen in the case of multiple choice tests to the matching test and so on.
4. They do not help to develop any literary qualities such as reasoning, paragraphing, logical coherence of ideas which are very necessary for social topics. A good and logical expression of ideas and how to present them through an essay type examination and it is not something unimportant.
5. These tests cannot develop the power of thinking, reasoning and judgement of the students of Social Studies, which are very essential in a democratic country like India.

OBJECTIVE TYPE TESTS

Evaluation is the last phase of teaching process. Its concern is to find out how far we have succeeded in achieving the goals set. For evaluation many types of tests are administered. These are: (A) Oral test; (B) written test; (C) Practical test. Of these the written test is the most important one. Under it we can have three types of tests.

1. Essay Type Tests
2. Short Answer Type Tests.
3. Objective Type Tests.

1. **Essay Type Tests.** In it examinees are asked to write essays on some topics. For example:

   Q. "Point out the importance of iron/steel in the advancement of Culture."

   OR

   What were the causes of discontent against the English in India.

   Answer to such questions are required to be given in 150 words or so.

2. **Short Answer Type Tests.** The answers to the questions are brief and there is clarity in them The Essay Type and Objective Type Tests have their own limitations. But short answer question adopts the middle path. It is expected of the pupils to answer a question in eight to ten lines. For example:

   Q. Why did the first war of independence fail?

   OR

   Write the drawbacks of the caste system.

3. **Objective Type Tests.** As a result of the bitter criticism of Essay Type Tests emphasis came to be put on Objective Type Tests in the educational world. The Objective Type Questions are based upon actual state. Pupils have no freedom in answering them, because every question has specific answer and it is expected of the pupils to give that very specific answer.

If he answers differently, then it is considered as wrong. The answers are so pithy as to write a word or to draw a line under a sentence and it serves the purpose alright. In such a test, nearly one hundred questions can be answered within an hour.

MERITS AND CHARACTERISTICS OF OBJECTIVE TYPE TESTS

The merits and specialities teaching of Social Studies/Science are as under:

1. There is no importance given to handwriting or the speed of writing or the views of the examiner. So, they are more reliable, standardised and objective.
2. These cover the maximum part of the syllabus.
3. There is no room for guess work since instructions are clear for all.
4. It is easy to give answers and quickly too, objectively and with reliability.
5. These are free from the impact of language style and it removes the influence of mood.

6. These discourage learning by the short memory but develop in pupils qualities like thinking, observations, probe etc.
7. It requires less of writing and is less exhausting.
8. From economic point also, it is highly useful as it does not cost much.
9. It saves time since the answer is brief and definite.
10. Language weakness does not hinder in giving answers.

DEMERITS AND LIMITATIONS OF OBJECTIVE TYPE TESTS

1. This type of test cannot measure the full knowledge of every subject.
2. It tests only knowledge aspect of his ability *i.e.*, knowledge about facts.
3. It encourages copying tendency.
4. The questions cannot be easily framed. It requires lot of time and labour for this work.
5. The chances of making guess increases in answering the questions.
6. The language ability and expression of feelings cannot be ascertained. There is no test for linguistic style and expression.
7. It does not develop originality and creativity in pupils.
8. Pupils do not come to know about their linguistic weaknesses.
9. The development of knowledge of pupils takes place in a piece meal manner. There is no sequence in these pieces.
10. No importance given to good hand and so it becomes illegible.

SUGGESTIONS FOR IMPROVEMENT OF OBJECTIVE TYPE TESTS

The following suggestions should be borne in mind while framing objective type questions:

1. Questions should be related to aims.
2. These should be framed as to leave no room for guess work.
3. Validity and reliability should be ensured as far as possible.
4. Answers to the questions should be definite.
5. The number of questions should be fixed aspire time duration available.
6. Attention should be paid to level of toughness of questions.
7. With every type of question the direction given should be clear and exact.

COMPARATIVE STUDY OF OBJECTIVE TYPE AND ESSAY TYPE TESTS

Essay Type Test	*Objective Type Test*
1. The number of questions is very less. Ordinarily five questions solved in three hours.	1. The number of questions is very large. Ordinarily 80 questions to 120 questions to be attempted in one or 1½ hour time.
2. It is easy to set questions.	2. Framing of questions is a difficult task.
3. Questions are based upon some parts of the syllabus.	3. Questions are based on entire syllabus.
4. Evaluation of limited areas of the subject-matter is possible.	4. Evaluation of vast areas of syllabus is possible.
5. Nature of answers to questions is uncertain, unlimited and essay type and difference of opinions arise in their evaluation. The award depends upon the examiner.	5. The nature of answers to questions is limited, certain and exact and there is no difference of opinion in their evaluation.
6. There is scope for answering in an original way. There are glimpses in their answers of imagination.	6. Barring re-call questions for answering the pupils have to select answer from the alternatives only. No opportunity for expressing originality.

Contd.

Essay Type Test	*Objective Type Test*
7. Without any hesitation he can freely express his views and feelings. This enables evaluation of his handwriting and language style.	7. No idea can be had of pupils attitude for expression and language aspect *i.e.*, no test for language, style and expression.
8. This develops the habit of memorising things.	8. It encourages copying tendencies.
9. There is no scope for guessing answers.	9. There is lot of scope for guess work in answering.
10. It takes much labour and time for the examiner to evaluate answers.	10. As compared with essay type test, it takes less time and labour.

EXAMPLES THE VARIOUS OBJECTIVES TYPE TESTS

Objective Type Test is generally a modified form of tests conducted by teachers. In it, questions are set which have brief answers. We can call them as New Objective Type Tests. These are of two types.

1. Recognition Test. The ability to recognition is tested. We can divide such questions under five heads, which are as under:

(A) TRUE-FALSE OR YES-NO FORM

Put mark (✓) against the statement which is correct and the mark (×) against which is false. For example:

1. The Prime Minister of India is Sh. Venkat Raman. (×)
2. Jamindari system suits Indians. (×)
3. The origin of Indian Culture is found in the Aryan Civilisation. ( )
4. The world tension can be reduced not by the Panchsheel but by atom war. (×)

Write 'Yes' if the statement is correct and 'No' if it is false.

1. Guru Nanak was the founder of the Bhakti Culture. Yes/No
2. In ancient time agriculture was the chief profession of the people. Yes/No

3. Aurangzeb was a tolerant ruler. Yes/No
4. The High Court of Haryana is located in Chandigarh. Yes/No

(B) MULTIPLE CHOICE

In such test statement is left incomplete and next are given three to four answers. But to complete the sentence, only one out the given answers is to be there. The pupils have to find out the correct answer: For example:

1. The first war of independence (1857) was unsuccessful because:
   (i) Many Indians did not like it.
   (ii) Many Indians liked the English rule.
   (iii) It was not properly planned.
2. During the reign of Ashoka Buddhism spread because:
   (i) The ascetic took a lot of interest.
   (ii) Lord Buddha died.
   (iii) It was a state religion.
   (iv) People very much liked its principles.
3. The capital of India is:
   (i) Mumbai
   (ii) Chennai
   (iii) Delhi
   (iv) Shimla

We can call it the best answer test also for example: The food problem in India is because:

(i) Food stuff in India is greatly wasted.
(ii) The population in India as increasing quite rapidly.
(iii) The modes of cultivation in India are out-dated.
(iv) The government is indifferent for solving it.

(C) MATCHING TEST

There are two columns in it. The one contains statements and the other its answers. Pupils are asked to match the statements with their correct answers. For example:

Cities	*Industry*
Jagadhri	Cycle parts
Chittaranjan	Woollen Cloth
Ludhiana	Jute Mills
Dhariwal	Paper
Bhilai	Manure
Kolkata	Steel
Sindri	Rly. Engines

2. Recall Test. It tests memory. The questions can be divided into two parts.

1. ***Simple Recalls.*** The recollection of the pupils is tested. It helps in testing their recollecting power about events, facts etc.

   This testing can be done as under:

   (i) When was the East India Company established?

   (ii) When was the Constitution of India adopted?

   (iii) Which one is the biggest river in India?

   (iv) When did Lal Bahadur Shastri meet his death?

2. **Completion Test.** The questions are given bearing blanks in them. The pupils are to fill in with appropriate words. For example:

   (i) The President appoints the leader of the majority party in the Lok Sabha as..................

   (ii) The President of India is ....

   (iii) Prime Minister of India is...............

MODEL QUESTION PAPER ON SOCIAL STUDIES FOR IX CLASS

A. Question Nos. from 1 to 6 may be answered in one word or a sentence.

1. In what form the early man developed?
2. When did the iron age start?

3. Where did agriculture start in Africa?
4. Which new social and economic organisations came into being in Europe in medieval period?
5. When and who invented telephone?
6. To which country Bismarck belonged?

B. Answer to Question Nos. 7 to 12 each be given in not more than 50 words. Each question carries three marks.

7. How did community life evolve?
8. What reforms were introduced in agriculture under ancient civilisations?
9. Write defects of caste system.
10. What was the effect of the British Industrial revolution on India?
11. What were the causes responsible for the down-fall of the Roman Civilisation?
12. What were the obstacles in respect of unification of Italy?
13. In the outline map of the world, show the areas of any four civilisation.

Question Nos. 14 and 15 be answered in not more than 50 words.

14. Point out the importance of iron in the growth of civilisation.

    OR

    Describe the European Social classes at the time of feudalism. What new class developed and why, in the last years of the medieval period?
15. What do you mean by renaissance? What were its causes?

CIVICS

D. Question Nos. from 16 to 20 be answered in one word or a sentence.

16. Define a Joint Family.
17. What is the difference in the working of the legislature and the executive?
18. What is the lingua franca of India?
19. To which religion majority of the people in India belong.
20. What is meant by secularism?
21. What is meant by socialism.

E. Questions Nos. 22 to 25 be answered in not more than 40 words.

22. Who is a citizen? How do they differ from the aliens?'
23. What sort of government is there in India? Why have we adopted it?
24. Describe four solutions to eradicate untouchability.
25. India is a rich country, but her people are poor, Why?

F. Question No. 26 be answered in not more than 150 words.

26. Describe the obstacles coming in the way of national integration.

OR

What do you understand by Joint Family? What are the factors accounting for the decline of this system?

Moffatt writes about evaluation, "The task of evaluation, to be accomplished, is more complex in the process of evaluation in Social Studies that, in other subjects. It is because, in Social Studies the tests regarding understanding, tendencies in behaviour, habits and ideals for development, by the teacher is more complex. So the Social Studies teacher need the acquainted with various methods, techniques, and tests, along with their forms and administration in evaluation."

❑